THE STORY OF A ROUND-HOUSE
AND OTHER POEMS

THE MACMILLAN COMPANY
NEW YORK · BOSTON · CHICAGO · DALLAS
ATLANTA · SAN FRANCISCO

MACMILLAN & CO., Limited
LONDON · BOMBAY · CALCUTTA
MELBOURNE

THE MACMILLAN CO. OF CANADA, Ltd.
TORONTO

THE STORY OF
A ROUND–HOUSE AND
OTHER POEMS

BY

JOHN MASEFIELD

AUTHOR OF " THE EVERLASTING MERCY "
" THE WIDOW IN THE BYE STREET," ETC.

NEW AND REVISED EDITION

New York
THE MACMILLAN COMPANY
1913

J.C. Humanities

45666

DEC 3 1943

PR
6000
M39657

Norwood Press
J. S. Cushing Co. — Berwick & Smith Co.
Norwood, Mass., U.S.A.

13-15276

CONTENTS

THE STORY OF A ROUND-HOUSE
AND OTHER POEMS

DAUBER

I

FOUR bells were struck, the watch was called
on deck,
All work aboard was over for the hour,
And some men sang and others played
at check,
Or mended clothes or watched the sunset
glower.
The bursting west was like an opening
flower,
And one man watched it till the light was
dim,
But no one went across to talk to him.

He was the painter in that swift ship's
crew,
Lampman and painter — tall, a slight-built
man,

Young for his years, and not yet twenty-
    two;
Sickly, and not yet brown with the sea's tan.
Bullied and damned at since the voyage
    began,
"Being neither man nor seaman by his
    tally,"
He bunked with the idlers just abaft the
    galley.

His work began at five; he worked all day,
Keeping no watch and having all night in.
His work was what the mate might care to
    say;
He mixed red lead in many a bouilli tin;
His dungarees were smeared with paraffin.
"Go drown himself" his round-house mates
    advised him,
And all hands called him "Dauber" and
    despised him.

Si, the apprentice, stood beside the spar,
Stripped to the waist, a basin at his side,
Slushing his hands to get away the tar,
And then he washed himself and rinsed and
      dried;
Towelling his face, hair-towzelled, eager
      eyed,
He crossed the spar to Dauber, and there
      stood
Watching the gold of heaven turn to blood.

They stood there by the rail while the swift
      ship
Tore on out of the tropics, straining her
      sheets,
Whitening her trackway to a milky strip,
Dim with green bubbles and twisted water
      meets,
Her clacking tackle tugged at pins and
      cleats,

Her great sails bellied stiff, her great masts
    leaned :
They watched how the seas struck and burst
    and greened.

Si talked with Dauber, standing by the
    side.
"Why did you come to sea, painter?" he
    said.
"I want to be a painter," he replied,
"And know the sea and ships from A to Z,
And paint great ships at sea before I'm dead ;
Ships under skysails running down the
    Trade —
Ships and the sea ; there's nothing finer
    made.

"But there's so much to learn, with sails
    and ropes,
And how the sails look, full or being furled,

And how the lights change in the troughs
    and slopes,
And the sea's colours up and down the
    world,
And how a storm looks when the sprays
    are hurled
High as the yard (they say) I want to see;
There's none ashore can teach such things
    to me.

"And then the men and rigging, and the way
Ships move, running or beating, and the
    poise
At the roll's end, the checking in the sway —
I want to paint them perfect, short of the
    noise;
And then the life, the half-decks full of boys,
The fo'c'sles with the men there, dripping
    wet:
I know the subjects that I want to get.

"It's not been done, the sea, not yet been
        done,
From the inside, by one who really knows ;
I'd give up all if I could be the one,
But art comes dear the way the money
        goes.
So I have come to sea, and I suppose
Three years will teach me all I want to learn
And make enough to keep me till I earn."

Even as he spoke his busy pencil moved,
Drawing the leap of water off the side
Where the great clipper trampled iron-
        hooved,
Making the blue hills of the sea divide,
Shearing a glittering scatter in her stride,
And leaping on full tilt with all sails draw-
        ing,
Proud as a war-horse, snuffing battle, paw-
        ing.

"I cannot get it yet — not yet," he said;
"That leap and light, and sudden change
    to green,
And all the glittering from the sunset's red,
And the milky colours where the bursts
    have been,
And then the clipper striding like a queen
Over it all, all beauty to the crown.
I see it all, I cannot put it down.

"It's hard not to be able. There, look
    there!
I cannot get the movement nor the light;
Sometimes it almost makes a man despair
To try and try and never get it right.
Oh, if I could — oh, if I only might,
I wouldn't mind what hells I'd have to
    pass,
Not if the whole world called me fool and
    ass."

Down sank the crimson sun into the sea,

The wind cut chill at once, the west grew
dun.

"Out sidelights!" called the mate. "Hi,
where is he?"

The Boatswain called, "Out sidelights, damn
you! Run!"

"He's always late or lazing," murmured
one —

"The Dauber, with his sketching." Soon
the tints

Of red and green passed on dark water-
glints.

Darker it grew, still darker, and the stars

Burned golden, and the fiery fishes came.

The wire-note loudened from the straining
spars;

The sheet-blocks clacked together always
the same;

The rushing fishes streaked the seas with
      flame,
Racing the one speed noble as their own:
What unknown joy was in those fish un-
      known!

Just by the round-house door, as it grew dark,
The Boatswain caught the Dauber with,
      "Now, you;
Till now I've spared you, damn you! now
      you hark:
I've just had hell for what you didn't do;
I'll have you broke and sent among the
      crew
If you get me more trouble by a particle.
Don't you forget, you daubing, useless
      article!

"You thing, you twice-laid thing from Port
      Mahon!"

Then came the Cook's "Is that the Dauber
    there ?

Why don't you leave them stinking paints
    alone ?

They stink the house out, poisoning all the air.

Just take them out." "Where to ?" "I
    don't care where.

I won't have stinking paint here." From
    their plates :

"That's right ; wet paint breeds fever,"
    growled his mates.

He took his still wet drawings from the
    berth

And climbed the ladder to the deck-house
    top ;

Beneath, the noisy half-deck rang with mirth,

For two ship's boys were putting on the
    strop :

One, clambering up to let the skylight drop,

Saw him bend down beneath a boat and lay
His drawings there, till all were hid away,

And stand there silent, leaning on the boat,
Watching the constellations rise and burn,
Until the beauty took him by the throat,
So stately is their glittering overturn;
Armies of marching eyes, armies that yearn
With banners rising and falling, and pass-
     ing by
Over the empty silence of the sky.

The Dauber sighed there looking at the sails,
Wind-steadied arches leaning on the night,
The high trucks traced on heaven and left
     no trails;
The moonlight made the topsails almost
     white,
The passing sidelight seemed to drip green
     light.

And on the clipper rushed with fire-bright
    bows;
He sighed, "I'll never do't," and left the
    house.

"Now," said the reefer, "up! Come, Sam;
    come, Si,
Dauber's been hiding something." Up they
    slid,
Treading on naked tiptoe stealthily
To grope for treasure at the long-boat skid.
"Drawings!" said Sam. "Is this what
    Dauber hid?
Lord! I expected pudding, not this rot.
Still, come, we'll have some fun with what
    we've got."

They smeared the paint with turpentine
    until
They could remove with mess-clouts every
    trace

Of quick perception caught by patient
skill,
And lines that had brought blood into his
face.
They wiped the pigments off, and did erase,
With knives, all sticking clots. When they
had done.
Under the boat they laid them every one.

All he had drawn since first he came to sea,
His six weeks' leisure fruits, they laid them
there.
They chuckled then to think how mad
he'd be
Finding his paintings vanished into air.
Eight bells were struck, and feet from
everywhere
Went shuffling aft to muster in the dark;
The mate's pipe glowed above, a dim red
spark.

Names in the darkness passed and voices
    cried;

The red spark glowed and died, the faces
    seemed

As things remembered when a brain has
    died,

To all but high intenseness deeply dreamed.

Like hissing spears the fishes' fire streamed,

And on the clipper rushed with tossing
    mast,

A bath of flame broke round her as she
    passed.

The watch was set, the night came, and
    the men

Hid from the moon in shadowed nooks to
    sleep,

Bunched like the dead; still, like the dead,
    as when

Plague in a city leaves none even to weep.

The ship's track brightened to a mile-
    broad sweep;
The mate there felt her pulse, and eyed
    the spars:
South-west by south she staggered under
    the stars.

Down in his bunk the Dauber lay awake
Thinking of his unfitness for the sea.
Each failure, each derision, each mistake,
There in the life not made for such as he;
A morning grim with trouble sure to be,
A noon of pain from failure, and a night
Bitter with men's contemning and despite.

This in the first beginning, the green leaf,
Still in the Trades before bad weather fell;
What harvest would he reap of hate and
    grief
When the loud Horn made every life a hell?

When the sick ship lay over, clanging her
   bell,

And no time came for painting or for drawing,

But all hands fought, and icy death came
   clawing?

Hell, he expected, — hell. His eyes grew
   blind;

The snoring from his messmates droned
   and snuffled,

And then a gush of pity calmed his mind.

The cruel torment of his thought was
   muffled,

Without, on deck, an old, old, seaman
   shuffled,

Humming his song, and through the open
   door

A moonbeam moved and thrust along the
   floor.

The green bunk curtains moved, the brass
   rings clicked,
The Cook cursed in his sleep, turning and
   turning,
The moonbeams' moving finger touched
   and picked,
And all the stars in all the sky were burning.
"This is the art I've come for, and am
   learning,
The sea and ships and men and travelling
   things.
It is most proud, whatever pain it brings."

He leaned upon his arm and watched the
   light
Sliding and fading to the steady roll;
This he would some day paint, the ship
   at night,
And sleeping seamen tired to the soul;
   c

The space below the bunks as black as coal,
Gleams upon chests, upon the unlit lamp,
The ranging door hook, and the locker
　　clamp.

This he would paint, and that, and all these
　　scenes,
And proud ships carrying on, and men
　　their minds,
And blues of rollers toppling into greens,
And shattering into white that bursts and
　　blinds,
And scattering ships running erect like
　　hinds,
And men in oilskins beating down a sail
High on the yellow yard, in snow, in hail.

With faces ducked down from the slant-
　　ing drive
Of half-thawed hail mixed with half-frozen
　　spray,

The roaring canvas like a thing alive,
Shaking the mast, knocking their hands
away,
The foot-ropes jerking to the tug and sway,
The savage eyes salt-reddened at the rims,
And icicles on the south-wester brims.

And sunnier scenes would grow under his
brush,
The tropic dawn with all things dropping
dew,
The darkness and the wonder and the hush,
The insensate grey before the marvel grew;
Then the veil lifted from the trembling blue,
The walls of sky burst in, the flower, the
rose,
All the expanse of heaven a mind that glows.

He turned out of his bunk; the Cook still
tossed,

One of the other two spoke in his sleep.

A cockroach scuttled where the moonbeam
    crossed;

Outside there was the ship, the night, the
    deep.

"It is worth while," the youth said; "I
    will keep

To my resolve, I'll learn to paint all this.

My Lord, my God, how beautiful it is!"

Outside was the ship's rush to the wind's
    hurry,

A resonant wire-hum from every rope,

The broadening bow-wash in a fiery flurry,

The leaning masts in their majestic slope,

And all things strange with moonlight:
    filled with hope

By all that beauty going as man bade,

He turned and slept in peace. Eight bells
    were made.

II

Next day was Sunday, his free painting
　　day,
While the fine weather held, from eight
　　till eight.
He rose when called at five, and did array
The round-house gear, and set the kit-bags
　　straight;
Then kneeling down, like housemaid at a
　　grate,
He scrubbed the deck with sand until his
　　knees
Were blue with dye from his wet dungarees.

Soon all was clean, his Sunday tasks were
　　done;
His day was clear for painting as he chose.
The wetted decks were drying in the
　　sun,

The men coiled up, or swabbed, or sought
  repose.
The drifts of silver arrows fell and rose
As flying fish took wing; the breakfast
  passed,
Wasting good time, but he was free at last.

Free for two hours and more to tingle deep,
Catching a likeness in a line or tint,
The canvas running up in a proud sweep,
Wind-wrinkled at the clews, and white
  like lint,
The glittering of the blue waves into glint;
Free to attempt it all, the proud ship's
  pawings,
The sea, the sky — he went to fetch his
  drawings.

Up to the deck-house top he quickly
  climbed,

He stooped to find them underneath the
  boat.
He found them all obliterated, slimed,
Blotted, erased, gone from him line and
  note.
They were all spoiled: a lump came in his
  throat,
Being vain of his attempts, and tender
  skinned —
Beneath the skylight watching reefers
  grinned.

He clambered down, holding the ruined
  things.
"Bosun," he called, "look here, did you
  do these:
Wipe off my paints and cut them into
  strings,
And smear them till you can't tell chalk
  from cheese?

Don't stare, but did you do it? Answer,
　　please."

The Bosun turned: "I'll give you a thick
　　ear!

Do it? I didn't. Get to hell from here!

"I touch your stinking daubs? The
　　Dauber's daft."

A crowd was gathering now to hear the
　　fun;

The reefers tumbled out, the men laid aft,

The Cook blinked, cleaning a mess kid in
　　the sun.

"What's up with Dauber now?" said every-
　　one.

"Someone has spoiled my drawings — look
　　at this!"

"Well, that's a dirty trick, by God, it is!"

"It is," said Sam, "a low-down dirty trick,

To spoil a fellow's work in such a way,

And if you catch him, Dauber, punch him
sick,

For he deserves it, be he who he may."

A seaman shook his old head wise and grey.

"It seems to me," he said, "who ain't no
judge,

Them drawings look much better now
they're smudge."

"Where were they, Dauber? On the deck-
house? Where?"

"Under the long-boat, in a secret place."

"The blackguard must have seen you put
them there.

He is a swine! I tell him to his face:

I didn't think we'd anyone so base."

"Nor I," said Dauber. "There was six
weeks' time

Just wasted in these drawings: it's a crime!"

"Well, don't you say we did it," growled
    his mates,

"And as for crime, be damned ! the things
    were smears —

Best overboard, like you, with shot for
    weights ;

Thank God they're gone, and now go shake
    your ears."

The Dauber listened, very near to tears.

"Dauber, if I were you," said Sam again,

"I'd aft, and see the Captain and com-
    plain."

A sigh came from the assembled seamen
    there.

Would he be such a fool for their delight

As go to tell the Captain? Would he
    dare ?

And would the thunder roar, the lightning
    smite ?

There was the Captain come to take a sight,
Handling his sextant by the chart-house aft.
The Dauber turned, the seamen thought
    him daft.

The Captain took his sights — a mate be-
    low
Noted the times; they shouted to each
    other,
The Captain quick with "Stop," the answer
    slow,
Repeating slowly one height then another.
The swooping clipper stumbled through
    the smother,
The ladder brasses in the sunlight burned,
The Dauber waited till the Captain turned.

There stood the Dauber, humbled to the
    bone,
Waiting to speak. The Captain let him wait,

Glanced at the course, and called in even
    tone,

"What is the man there wanting, Mr.
    Mate?"
The logship clattered on the grating straight,
The reel rolled to the scuppers with a
    clatter,
The Mate came grim: "Well, Dauber,
    what's the matter?"

"Please, sir, they spoiled my drawings."
        "Who did?" "They."
"Who's they?" "I don't quite know, sir."
        "Don't quite know, sir?
Then why are you aft to talk about it, hey?
Whom d'you complain of?" "No one."
        "No one?" "No, sir."
"Well, then, go forward till you've found
    them. Go, sir.
If you complain of someone, then I'll see.

Now get to hell! and don't come bothering
    me."

"But, sir, they washed them off, and some
    they cut.
Look here, sir, how they spoiled them."
    "Never mind.
Go shove your head inside the scuttle butt,
And that will make you cooler.   You will find
Nothing like water when you're mad and
    blind.
Where were the drawings? in your chest,
    or where?"
"Under the long-boat, sir; I put them
    there."

"Under the long-boat, hey? Now mind
    your tip.
I'll have the skids kept clear with nothing
    round them;

The long-boat ain't a store in this here ship.

Lucky for you it wasn't I who found them.

If I had seen them, Dauber, I'd have drowned
    them.

Now you be warned by this.   I tell you
    plain —

Don't stow your brass-rags under boats
    again.

"Go forward to your berth."   The Dauber
    turned.

The listeners down below them winked and
    smiled,

Knowing how red the Dauber's temples
    burned,

Having lost the case about his only child.

His work was done to nothing and defiled,

And there was no redress : the Captain's voice

Spoke, and called "Painter," making him
    rejoice.

The Captain and the Mate conversed together.

"Drawings, you tell me, Mister?" "Yes,
sir; views:

Wiped off with turps, I gather that's his
blether.

He says they're things he can't afford to
lose.

He's Dick, who came to sea in dancing
shoes,

And found the dance a bear dance. They
were hidden

Under the long-boat's chocks, which I've
forbidden."

"Wiped off with turps?" The Captain
sucked his lip.

"Who did it, Mister?" "Reefers, I suppose;

Them devils do the most pranks in a ship;

The round-house might have done it, Cook
      or Bose.''

''I can't take notice of it till he knows.

How does he do his work?'' ''Well, no
      offence;

He tries; he does his best. He's got no
      sense.''

''Painter,'' the Captain called; the Dauber
      came.

''What's all this talk of drawings? What's
      the matter?''

''They spoiled my drawings, sir.'' ''Well,
      who's to blame?

The long-boat's there for no one to get at
      her;

You broke the rules, and if you choose to
      scatter

Gear up and down where it's no right to be,

And suffer as result, don't come to me.

"Your place is in the round-house, and
　　your gear
Belongs where you belong. Who spoiled
　　your things?
Find out who spoiled your things and fetch
　　him here."
"But, sir, they cut the canvas into strings."
"I want no argument nor questionings.
Go back where you belong and say no more,
And please remember that you're not on
　　shore."

The Dauber touched his brow and slunk
　　away —
They eyed his going with a bitter eye.
"Dauber," said Sam, "what did the Cap-
　　tain say?"
The Dauber drooped his head without
　　reply.
"Go forward, Dauber, and enjoy your cry."

D

The Mate limped to the rail; like little
feet

Over his head the drumming reef-points
beat.

The Dauber reached the berth and entered
in.

Much mockery followed after as he went,

And each face seemed to greet him with
the grin

Of hounds hot following on a creature
spent.

"Aren't you a fool?" each mocking visage
meant.

"Who did it, Dauber? What did Captain
say?

It is a crime, and there'll be hell to pay."

He bowed his head, the house was full of
smoke;

The Sails was pointing shackles on his chest.

"Lord, Dauber, be a man and take a
    joke" —

He puffed his pipe — "and let the matter
    rest.

Spit brown, my son, and get a hairy breast;

Get shoulders on you at the crojick braces,

And let this painting business go to blazes.

"What good can painting do to anyone?

I don't say never do it; far from that —

No harm in sometimes painting just for
    fun.

Keep it for fun, and stick to what you're
    at.

Your job's to fill your bones up and get
    fat;

Rib up like Barney's bull, and thick your
    neck.

Throw paints to hell, boy; you belong on
    deck."

"That's right," said Chips; "it's down-
 right good advice.

Painting's no good; what good can painting do

Up on a lower topsail stiff with ice,

With all your little fish-hooks frozen blue?

Painting won't help you at the weather
 clew,

Nor pass your gaskets for you, nor make
 sail.

Painting's a balmy job not worth a nail."

The Dauber did not answer; time was passing.

He pulled his easel out, his paints, his stool.

The wind was dropping, and the sea was
 glassing —

New realms of beauty waited for his rule;

The draught out of the crojick kept him
 cool.

He sat to paint, alone and melancholy.
"No turning fools," the Chips said, "from
    their folly."

He dipped his brush and tried to fix a line,
And then came peace, and gentle beauty came,
Turning his spirit's water into wine,
Lightening his darkness with a touch of
    flame:
O, joy of trying for beauty, ever the same,
You never fail, your comforts never end;
O, balm of this world's way; O, perfect
    friend!

III

THEY lost the Trades soon after; then
    came calm,
Light little gusts and rain, which soon in-
    creased

To glorious northers shouting out a psalm
At seeing the bright blue water silver
  fleeced;
Hornwards she rushed, trampling the seas
  to yeast.
There fell a rain-squall in a blind day's end
When for an hour the Dauber found a
  friend.

Out of the rain the voices called and passed,
The stay-sails flogged, the tackle yanked
  and shook.
Inside the harness-room a lantern cast
Light and wild shadows as it ranged its
  hook.
The watch on deck was gathered in the
  nook,
They had taken shelter in that secret place,
Wild light gave wild emotions to each
  face.

One beat the beef-cask, and the others sang

A song that had brought anchors out of
seas

In ports where bells of Christians never
rang,

Nor any sea mark blazed among the trees.

By forlorn swamps, in ice, by windy keys,

That song had sounded; now it shook the
air

From these eight wanderers brought together there.

Under the poop-break, sheltering from
the rain,

The Dauber sketched some likeness of
the room,

A note to be a prompting to his brain,

A spark to make old memory reillume.

"Dauber," said someone near him in the
gloom,

"How goes it, Dauber?" It was reefer
Si.
"There's not much use in trying to keep
dry."

They sat upon the sail-room doorway coam-
ing,
The lad held forth like youth, the Dauber
listened
To how the boy had had a taste for roam-
ing,
And what the sea is said to be and isn't.
Where the dim lamplight fell the wet deck
glistened.
Si said the Horn was still some weeks away,
"But tell me, Dauber, where d'you hail
from?   Eh?"

The rain blew past and let the stars appear;
The seas grew larger as the moonlight grew;

For half an hour the ring of heaven was
     clear,
Dusty with moonlight, grey rather than
     blue;
In that great moon the showing stars were
     few.
The sleepy time-boy's feet passed overhead.
"I come from out past Gloucester," Dauber
     said;

"Not far from Pauntley, if you know those
     parts;
The place is Spital Farm, near Silver Hill,
Above a trap-hatch where a mill-stream
     starts.
We had the mill once, but we've stopped
     the mill;
My dad and sister keep the farm on still.
We're only tenants, but we've rented there,
Father and son, for over eighty year.

"Father has worked the farm since grand-
          fer went;
It means the world to him; I can't think
          why.
They bleed him to the last half-crown for
          rent,
And this and that have almost milked him
          dry.
The land's all starved; if he'd put money
          by,
And corn was up, and rent was down two-
          thirds. . . .
But then they aren't, so what's the use of
          words.

"Yet still he couldn't bear to see it pass
To strangers, or to think a time would come
When other men than us would mow the
          grass,
And other names than ours have the home.

Some sorrows come from evil thought,
but some
Comes when two men are near, and both are
blind
To what is generous in the other's mind.

"I was the only boy, and father thought
I'd farm the Spital after he was dead,
And many a time he took me out and taught
About manures and seed-corn white and
red,
And soils and hops, but I'd an empty head ;
Harvest or seed, I would not do a turn —
I loathed the farm, I didn't want to learn.

"He did not mind at first, he thought it
youth
Feeling the collar, and that I should change.
Then time gave him some inklings of the
truth,

And that I loathed the farm, and wished
    to range.
Truth to a man of fifty's always strange;
It was most strange and terrible to him
That I, his heir, should be the devil's limb.

"Yet still he hoped the Lord might change
    my mind.
I'd see him bridle-in his wrath and hate,
And almost break my heart he was so kind,
Biting his lips sore with resolve to wait.
And then I'd try awhile; but it was Fate:
I didn't want to learn; the farm to me
Was mire and hopeless work and misery.

"Though there were things I loved about
    it, too —
The beasts, the apple-trees, and going hay-
    ing.
And then I tried; but no, it wouldn't do,

The farm was prison, and my thoughts
were straying.

And there'd come father, with his grey head,
praying,

'O, my dear son, don't let the Spital pass;

It's my old home, boy, where your grand-
fer was.

"'And now you won't learn farming; you
don't care.

The old home's nought to you. I've tried
to teach you;

I've begged Almighty God, boy, all I dare,

To use His hand if word of mine won't
reach you.

Boy, for your granfer's sake I do beseech
you,

Don't let the Spital pass to strangers.
Squire

Has said he'd give it you if we require.

"'Your mother used to walk here, boy,
    with me;

It was her favourite walk down to the mill;

And there we'd talk how little death would be,

Knowing our work was going on here still.

You've got the brains, you only want the
    will —

Don't disappoint your mother and your
    father.

I'll give you time to travel, if you'd rather.'

"But, no, I'd wander up the brooks to read.

Then sister Jane would start with nagging
    tongue,

Saying my sin made father's heart to bleed,

And how she feared she'd live to see me
    hung.

And then she'd read me bits from Dr. Young.

And when we three would sit to supper, Jane

Would fillip dad till dad began again.

"'I've been here all my life, boy. I was born

Up in the room above — looks on the mead.

I never thought you'd cockle my clean corn,

And leave the old home to a stranger's seed.

Father and I have made here 'thout a weed:

We've give our lives to make that. Eighty years.

And now I go down to the grave in tears.'

"And then I'd get ashamed and take off coat,

And work maybe a week, ploughing and sowing

And then I'd creep away and sail my boat,

Or watch the water when the mill was going.

That's my delight — to be near water flow-
     ing,
Dabbling or sailing boats or jumping stanks,
Or finding moorhens' nests along the
     banks.

"And one day father found a ship I'd
     built;
He took the cart-whip to me over that,
And I, half mad with pain, and sick with
     guilt,
Went up and hid in what we called the flat,
A dusty hole given over to the cat.
She kittened there; the kittens had worn
     paths
Among the cobwebs, dust, and broken
     laths.

"And putting down my hand between the
     beams

I felt a leathery thing, and pulled it clear:

A book with white cocoons stuck in the
seams.

Where spiders had had nests for many a
year.

It was my mother's sketch-book; hid, I
fear,

Lest dad should ever see it. Mother's life

Was not her own while she was father's
wife.

"There were her drawings, dated, pencilled
faint.

March was the last one, eighteen eighty-
three,

Unfinished that, for tears had smeared the
paint.

The rest was landscape, not yet brought
to be.

That was a holy afternoon to me;

E

That book a sacred book; the flat a place
Where I could meet my mother face to face.

"She had found peace of spirit, mother
          had,
Drawing the landscape from the attic there —
Heart-broken, often, after rows with dad,
Hid like a wild thing in a secret lair.
That rotting sketch-book showed me how
          and where
I, too, could get away; and then I knew
That drawing was the work I longed to do.

"Drawing became my life.   I drew, I
          toiled,
And every penny I could get I spent
On paints and artist's matters, which I
          spoiled
Up in the attic to my heart's content,
Till one day father asked me what I meant;

The time had come, he said, to make an
    end.
Now it must finish: what did I intend?

"Either I took to farming, like his son,
In which case he would teach me, early
    and late
(Provided that my daubing mood was done),
Or I must go: it must be settled straight.
If I refused to farm, there was the gate.
I was to choose, his patience was all gone,
The present state of things could not go on.

"Sister was there; she eyed me while he
    spoke.
The kitchen clock ran down and struck the
    hour,
And something told me father's heart was
    broke,
For all he stood so set and looked so sour.

Jane took a duster, and began to scour
A pewter on the dresser; she was crying.
I stood stock still a long time, not replying.

"Dad waited, then he snorted and turned
        round.
'Well, think of it,' he said.   He left the room,
His boots went clop along the stony ground
Out to the orchard and the apple-bloom.
A cloud came past the sun and made a
        gloom;
I swallowed with dry lips, then sister turned.
She was dead white but for her eyes that
        burned.

"'You're breaking father's heart, Joe,' she
        began;
'It's not as if ——' she checked, in too
        much pain.
'O, Joe, don't help to kill so fine a man;

You're giving him our mother over again.

It's wearing him to death, Joe, heart and
     brain;

You know what store he sets on leaving
     this

To (it's too cruel) — to a son of his.

"'Yet you go painting all the day. O,
     Joe,

Couldn't you make an effort? Can't you
     see

What folly it is of yours? It's not as
     though

You are a genius or could ever be.

O, Joe, for father's sake, if not for me,

Give up this craze for painting, and be wise

And work with father, where your duty
     lies.'

"'It goes too deep,' I said; 'I loathe the
     farm;

I couldn't help, even if I'd the mind.

Even if I helped, I'd only do him harm;

Father would see it, if he were not blind.

I was not built to farm, as he would find.

O, Jane, it's bitter hard to stand alone

And spoil my father's life or spoil my own.'

"'Spoil both,' she said, 'the way you're
        shaping now.

You're only a boy not knowing your own
        good.

Where will you go, suppose you leave here?
        How

Do you propose to earn your daily food?

Draw?   Daub the pavements?   There's
        a feckless brood

Goes to the devil daily, Joe, in cities

Only from thinking how divine their wit is.

"'Clouds are they, without water, carried
        away.

And you'll be one of them, the way you're
     going,
Daubing at silly pictures all the day,
And praised by silly fools who're always
     blowing.
And you choose this when you might go
     a-sowing,
Casting the good corn into chosen mould
That shall in time bring forth a hundred-
     fold.'

"So we went on, but in the end it ended.
I felt I'd done a murder; I felt sick.
There's much in human minds cannot be
     mended,
And that, not I, played dad a cruel trick.
There was one mercy: that it ended quick.
I went to join my mother's brother: he
Lived down the Severn.   He was kind to
     me.

"And there I learned house-painting for
    a living.
I'd have been happy there, but that I knew
I'd sinned before my father past for-
    giving,
And that they sat at home, that silent two,
Wearing the fire out and the evening
    through,
Silent, defeated, broken, in despair,
My plate unset, my name gone, and my
    chair.

"I saw all that; and sister Jane came
    white —
White as a ghost, with fiery, weeping
    eyes.
I saw her all day long and half the night,
Bitter as gall, and passionate and wise.
'Joe, you have killed your father: there
    he lies.

You have done your work — you with our
    mother's ways.'
She said it plain, and then her eyes would
    blaze.

"And then one day I had a job to do
Down below bridge, by where the docks
    begin,
And there I saw a clipper towing through,
Up from the sea that morning, entering in.
Raked to the nines she was, lofty and thin,
Her ensign ruffling red, her bunts in pile,
Beauty and strength together, wonder, style.

"She docked close to the gates, and there
    she lay
Over the water from me, well in sight;
And as I worked I watched her all the day,
Finding her beauty ever fresh delight.
Her house-flag was bright green with strips
    of white;

High in the sunny air it rose to shake
Above the skysail poles' most splendid
  rake.

"And when I felt unhappy I would look
Over the river at her; and her pride,
So calm, so quiet, came as a rebuke
To half the passionate pathways which I
  tried;
And though the autumn ran its term and
  died,
And winter fell and cold December came,
She was still splendid there, and still the
  same.

"Then on a day she sailed; but when she
  went
My mind was clear on what I had to try:
To see the sea and ships, and what they
  meant,

That was the thing I longed to do; so I

Drew and worked hard, and studied and put
    by,

And thought of nothing else but that one
    end,

But let all else go hang — love, money,
    friend.

"And now I've shipped as Dauber I've
    begun.

It was hard work to find a dauber's berth;

I hadn't any friends to find me one,

Only my skill, for what it may be worth;

But I'm at sea now, going about the earth,

And when the ship's paid off, when we re-
    turn,

I'll join some Paris studio and learn."

He stopped, the air came moist, Si did not
    speak;

The Dauber turned his eyes to where he
    sat,
Pressing the sail-room hinges with his
    cheek,
His face half covered with a drooping
    hat.
Huge dewdrops from the stay-sails dropped
    and spat.
Si did not stir, the Dauber touched his
    sleeve;
A little birdlike noise came from a sheave.

Si was asleep, sleeping a calm deep sleep,
Still as a warden of the Egyptian dead
In some old haunted temple buried deep
Under the desert sand, sterile and red.
The Dauber shook his arm; Si jumped and
    said,
"Good yarn, I swear! I say, you have a
    brain —

Was that eight bells that went?" He
    slept again.

Then waking up, "I've had a nap," he cried.
"Was that one bell? What, Dauber, you
    still here?"
"Si there?" the Mate's voice called. "Sir,"
    he replied.
The order made the lad's thick vision clear;
A something in the Mate's voice made him
    fear.
"Si," said the Mate, "I hear you've made
    a friend —
Dauber, in short. That friendship's got
    to end.

"You're a young gentleman. Your place
    aboard
Is with the gentlemen abaft the mast.
You're learning to command; you can't
    afford

To yarn with any man. But there . . .
    it's past.

You've done it once; let this time be the
    last.

The Dauber's place is forward. Do it
    again,

I'll put you bunking forward with the men.

"Dismiss." Si went, but Sam, beside the
    Mate,

Timekeeper there, walked with him to the
    rail

And whispered him the menace of "You
    wait" —

Words which have turned full many a reefer
    pale.

The watch was changed; the watch on deck
    trimmed sail.

Sam, going below, called all the reefers
    down,

Sat in his bunk and eyed them with a frown.

"Si here," he said, "has soiled the half-
    deck's name
Talking to Dauber — Dauber, the ship's
    clout.
A reefer takes the Dauber for a flame,
The half-deck take the round-house walking
    out.
He's soiled the half-deck's honour; now, no
    doubt,
The Bosun and his mates will come here
    sneaking,
Asking for smokes, or blocking gangways
    speaking.

"I'm not a vain man, given to blow or boast;
I'm not a proud man, but I truly feel
That while I've bossed this mess and ruled
    this roast

I've kept this hooker's half-deck damned
    genteel.
Si must ask pardon, or be made to squeal.
Down on your knees, dog; them we love
    we chasten.
Jao, pasea, my son — in English, Hasten."

Si begged for pardon, meekly kneeling
    down
Before the reefer's mess assembled grim.
The lamp above them smoked the glass all
    brown;
Beyond the door the dripping sails were
    dim.
The Dauber passed the door; none spoke
    to him.
He sought his berth and slept, or, waking,
    heard
Rain on the deck-house — rain, no other
    word.

IV

OUT of the air a time of quiet came,
Calm fell upon the heaven like a drouth;
The brass sky watched the brassy water
 flame.
Drowsed as a snail the clipper loitered south
Slowly, with no white bone across her
 mouth;
No rushing glory, like a queen made bold,
The Dauber strove to draw her as she
 rolled.

There the four leaning spires of canvas
 rose,
Royals and skysails lifting, gently lifting,
White like the brightness that a great fish
 blows
When billows are at peace and ships are
 drifting;
F

With mighty jerks that set the shadows
    shifting,

The courses tugged their tethers : a blue
    haze

Drifted like ghosts of flocks come down to
    graze.

There the great skyline made her perfect
    round,

Notched now and then by the sea's deeper
    blue ;

A smoke-smutch marked a steamer home-
    ward bound,

The haze wrought all things to intenser
    hue.

In tingling impotence the Dauber drew

As all men draw, keen to the shaken
    soul

To give a hint that might suggest the
    whole.

A naked seaman washing a red shirt
Sat at a tub whistling between his teeth;
Complaining blocks quavered like some-
thing hurt.
A sailor cut an old boot for a sheath,
The ship bowed to her shadow-ship beneath,
And little slaps of spray came at the roll
On to the deck-planks from the scupper-
hole.

He watched it, painting patiently, as
paints,
With eyes that pierce behind the blue sky's
veil,
The Benedictine in a Book of Saints
Watching the passing of the Holy Grail;
The green dish dripping blood, the trump,
the hail,
The spears that pass, the memory and the
passion,

The beauty moving under this world's
　　fashion.

But as he painted, slowly, man by man,
The seamen gathered near; the Bosun stood
Behind him, jeering; then the Sails began
Sniggering with comment that it was not
　　good.
Chips flicked his sketch with little scraps
　　of wood,
Saying, "That hit the top-knot," every
　　time.
Cook mocked, "My lovely drawings; it's
　　a crime."

Slowly the men came nearer, till a crowd
Stood at his elbow, muttering as he drew;
The Bosun, turning to them, spoke aloud,
"This is the ship that never got there.
　　　　You
Look at her here, what Dauber's trying to do.

Look at her ! lummy, like a Christmas-tree.

That thing's a ship ; he calls this painting.
    See ? "

Seeing the crowd, the Mate came forward ;
    then

"Sir," said the Bosun, "come and see the
    sight !

Here's Dauber makes a circus for the men.

He calls this thing a ship — this hell's
    delight !"

"Man," said the Mate, "you'll never get
    her right

Daubing like that.   Look here !"   He
    took a brush.

"Now, Dauber, watch ; I'll put you to the
    blush.

"Look here. Look there. Now watch this
    ship of mine."

He drew her swiftly from a memory stored.

"God, sir," the Bosun said, "you do her
    fine!"

"Ay," said the Mate, "I do so, by the Lord!

I'll paint a ship with any man aboard."

They hung about his sketch like beasts at
    bait.

"There now, I taught him painting," said
    the Mate.

When he had gone, the gathered men dis-
    persed;

Yet two or three still lingered to dispute

What errors made the Dauber's work
    the worst.

They probed his want of knowledge to the
    root.

"Bei Gott!" they swore, "der Dauber
    cannot do 't;

He haf no knolich how to put der pense.

Der Mate's is goot. Der Dauber haf no
    sense."

"You hear?" the Bosun cried, "you can-
    not do it!"
"A gospel truth," the Cook said, "true
    as hell!
And wisdom, Dauber, if you only knew it;
A five year boy would do a ship as well."
"If that's the kind of thing you hope to sell,
God help you," echoed Chips. "I tell
    you true,
The job's beyond you, Dauber; drop it,
    do.

"Drop it, in God's name drop it, and have
    done!
You see you cannot do it. Here's the
    Mate
Paints you to frazzles before everyone;

Paints you a dandy clipper while you wait.

While you, Lord love us, daub. I tell you
straight,

We've had enough of daubing; drop it; quit.

You cannot paint, so make an end of it."

"That's sense," said all; "you cannot, why
pretend?"

The Dauber rose and put his easel by.

"You've said enough," he said, "now let
it end.

Who cares how bad my painting may
be? I

Mean to go on, and, if I fail, to try.

However much I miss of my intent,

If I have done my best I'll be content.

"You cannot understand that. Let it be.

You cannot understand, nor know, nor
share.

This is a matter touching only me;

My sketch may be a daub, for aught I
care.

You may be right. But even if you were,

Your mocking should not stop this work
of mine;

Rot though it be, its prompting is divine.

"You cannot understand that — you, and
you,

And you, you Bosun. You can stand and
jeer,

That is the task your spirit fits you to,

That you can understand and hold most
dear.

Grin, then, like collars, ear to donkey ear,

But let me daub. Try, you, to understand

Which task will bear the light best on God's
hand."

V

THE wester came as steady as the Trades;
Brightly it blew, and still the ship did
    shoulder
The brilliance of the water's white cockades
Into the milky green of smoky smoulder.
The sky grew bluer and the air grew colder.
Southward she thundered while the westers
    held,
Proud, with taut bridles, pawing, but com-
    pelled.

And still the Dauber strove, though all men
    mocked,
To draw the splendour of the passing thing,
And deep inside his heart a something
    locked,
Long pricking in him, now began to sting —
A fear of the disasters storm might bring;

His rank as painter would be ended then —
He would keep watch and watch like other
men.

And go aloft with them to man the yard
When the great ship was rolling scuppers
under,
Burying her snout all round the compass
card,
While the green water struck at her and
stunned her ;
When the lee-rigging slacked, when one
long thunder
Boomed from the black to windward, when
the sail
Booted and spurred the devil in the gale

For him to ride on men : that was the
time
The Dauber dreaded ; then the test would
come,

When seas, half-frozen, slushed the decks
    with slime,
And all the air was blind with flying scum;
When the drenched sails were furled, when
    the fierce hum
In weather riggings died into the roar
Of God's eternal never tamed by shore.

Once in the passage he had worked aloft,
Shifting her suits one summer afternoon,
In the bright Trade wind, when the wind
    was soft,
Shaking the points, making the tackle
    croon.
But that was child's play to the future:
    soon
He would be ordered up when sails and
    spars
Were flying and going mad among the
    stars.

He had been scared that first time, daunted,
      thrilled,
Not by the height so much as by the size,
And then the danger to the man unskilled
In standing on a rope that runs through eyes.
"But in a storm," he thought, "the yards
      will rise
And roll together down, and snap their
      gear !"
The sweat came cold upon his palms for fear.

Sometimes in Gloucester he had felt a pang
Swinging below the house-eaves on a stage.
But stages carry rails; here he would hang
Upon a jerking rope in a storm's rage,
Ducked that the sheltering oilskin might
      assuage
The beating of the storm, clutching the
      jack,
Beating the sail, and being beaten back.

Drenched, frozen, gasping, blinded, beaten
     dumb,
High in the night, reeling great blinding
     arcs
As the ship rolled, his chappy fingers numb,
The deck below a narrow blur of marks,
The sea a welter of whiteness shot with
     sparks,
Now snapping up in bursts, now dying
     away,
Salting the horizontal snow with spray.

A hundred and fifty feet above the deck,
And there, while the ship rolls, boldly to
     sit
Upon a foot-rope moving, jerk and check,
While half a dozen seamen work on it;
Held by one hand, straining, by strength
     and wit
To toss a gasket's coil around the yard,

How could he compass that when blowing
    hard?

And if he failed in any least degree,
Or faltered for an instant, or showed slack,
He might go drown himself within the sea,
And add a bubble to the clipper's track.
He had signed his name, there was no turn-
    ing back,
No pardon for default — this must be done.
One iron rule at sea binds everyone.

Till now he had been treated with con-
    tempt
As neither man nor thing, a creature borne
On the ship's articles, but left exempt
From all the seamen's life except their
    scorn.
But he would rank as seaman off the Horn,
Work as a seaman, and be kept or cast
By standards set for men before the mast.

Even now they shifted suits of sails; they
    bent
The storm-suit ready for the expected time;
The mighty wester that the Plate had lent
Had brought them far into the wintry clime.
At dawn, out of the shadow, there was
    rime,
The dim Magellan Clouds were frosty clear,
The wind had edge, the testing-time was
    near.

And then he wondered if the tales were
    lies
Told by old hands to terrify the new,
For, since the ship left England, only
    twice
Had there been need to start a sheet or
    clew,
Then only royals, for an hour or two,
And no seas broke aboard, nor was it cold.

What were these gales of which the stories
    told?

The thought went by.   He had heard the
    Bosun tell
Too often, and too fiercely, not to know
That being off the Horn in June is hell:
Hell of continual toil in ice and snow,
Frostbitten hell in which the westers blow
Shrieking for days on end, in which the
    seas
Gulf the starved seamen till their marrows
    freeze.

Such was the weather he might look to
    find,
Such was the work expected: there re-
    mained
Firmly to set his teeth, resolve his mind,
And be the first, however much it pained,

G

And bring his honour round the Horn un-
     stained,
And win his mates' respect; and thence,
     untainted,
Be ranked as man however much he
     painted.

He drew deep breath; a gantline swayed
     aloft
A lower topsail, hard with rope and
     leather,
Such as men's frozen fingers fight with oft
Below the Ramirez in Cape Horn weather.
The arms upon the yard hove all together,
Lighting the head along; a thought occurred
Within the painter's brain like a bright
     bird:

That this, and so much like it, of man's
     toil,

Compassed by naked manhood in strange
    places,
Was all heroic, but outside the coil
Within which modern art gleams or grim-
    aces;
That if he drew that line of sailor's faces
Sweating the sail, their passionate play and
    change,
It would be new, and wonderful, and
    strange.

That that was what his work meant; it
    would be
A training in new vision — a revealing
Of passionate men in battle with the
    sea,
High on an unseen stage, shaking and
    reeling;
And men through him would understand
    their feeling,

Their might, their misery, their tragic
    power,
And all by suffering pain a little hour;

High on the yard with them, feeling their
    pain,
Battling with them; and it had not been
    done.
He was a door to new worlds in the brain,
A window opening letting in the sun,
A voice saying, "Thus is bread fetched
    and ports won,
And life lived out at sea where men exist
Solely by man's strong brain and sturdy
    wrist."

So he decided, as he cleaned his brasses,
Hearing without, aloft, the curse, the shout
Where the taut gantline passes and re-
    passes,

Heaving new topsails to be lighted out.

It was most proud, however self might
doubt,

To share man's tragic toil and paint it true.

He took the offered Fate: this he would
do.

That night the snow fell between six and
seven,

A little feathery fall so light, so dry —

An aimless dust out of a confused heaven,

Upon an air no steadier than a sigh;

The powder dusted down and wandered by

So purposeless, so many, and so cold,

Then died, and the wind ceased and the
ship rolled.

Rolled till she clanged — rolled till the
brain was tired,

Marking the acme of the heaves, the
pause

While the sea-beauty rested and respired,
Drinking great draughts of roller at her
　　hawse.
Flutters of snow came aimless upon flaws.
"Lock up your paints," the Mate said,
　　speaking light:
"This is the Horn; you'll join my watch
　　to-night!"

VI

ALL through the windless night the clipper
　　rolled
In a great swell with oily gradual heaves
Which rolled her down until her time-bells
　　tolled,
Clang, and the weltering water moaned
　　like beeves.
The thundering rattle of slatting shook the
　　sheaves,

Startles of water made the swing ports
     gush,
The sea was moaning and sighing and say-
     ing "Hush !"

It was all black and starless. Peering
     down
Into the water, trying to pierce the gloom,
One saw a dim, smooth, oily glitter of
     brown
Heaving and dying away and leaving
     room
For yet another.   Like the march of doom
Came those great powers of marching
     silences ;
Then fog came down, dead-cold, and hid
     the seas.

They set the Dauber to the foghorn.   There
He stood upon the poop, making to sound

Out of the pump the sailor's nasal blare,
Listening lest ice should make the note
 resound.
She bayed there like a solitary hound
Lost in a covert; all the watch she
 bayed.
The fog, come closelier down, no answer
 made.

Denser it grew, until the ship was lost.
The elemental hid her; she was merged
In mufflings of dark death, like a man's
 ghost,
New to the change of death, yet thither
 urged.
Then from the hidden waters something
 surged —
Mournful, despairing, great, greater than
 speech,
A noise like one slow wave on a still beach.

Mournful, and then again mournful, and
    still
Out of the night that mighty voice arose;
The Dauber at his foghorn felt the thrill.
Who rode that desolate sea? What forms
    were those?
Mournful, from things defeated, in the
    throes
Of memory of some conquered hunting-
    ground,
Out of the night of death arose the sound.

"Whales!" said the Mate. They stayed
    there all night long
Answering the horn. Out of the night
    they spoke,
Defeated creatures who had suffered wrong,
But were still noble underneath the stroke.
They filled the darkness when the Dauber
    woke;

The men came peering to the rail to hear,
And the sea sighed, and the fog rose up
    sheer.

A wall of nothing at the world's last edge,
Where no life came except defeated life.
The Dauber felt shut in within a hedge,
Behind which form was hidden and thought
    was rife,
And that a blinding flash, a thrust, a knife
Would sweep the hedge away and make
    all plain,
Brilliant beyond all words, blinding the
    brain.

So the night passed, but then no morning
    broke —
Only a something showed that night was
    dead.
A sea-bird, cackling like a devil, spoke,

And the fog drew away and hung like
    lead.

Like mighty cliffs it shaped, sullen and red;

Like glowering gods at watch it did ap-
    pear,

And sometimes drew away, and then drew
    near.

Like islands, and like chasms, and like hell,

But always mighty and red, gloomy and
    ruddy,

Shutting the visible sea in like a well;

Slow heaving in vast ripples, blank and
    muddy,

Where the sun should have risen it streaked
    bloody.

The day was still-born; all the sea-fowl
    scattering

Splashed the still water, mewing, hovering,
    clattering.

Then Polar snow came down little and
    light,
Till all the sky was hidden by the small,
Most multitudinous drift of dirty white
Tumbling and wavering down and covering
    all —
Covering the sky, the sea, the clipper tall,
Furring the ropes with white, casing the
    mast,
Coming on no known air, but blowing past.

And all the air seemed full of gradual
    moan,
As though in those cloud-chasms the horns
    were blowing
The mort for gods cast out and overthrown,
Or for the eyeless sun plucked out and
    going.
Slow the low gradual moan came in the
    snowing;

The Dauber felt the prelude had begun.
The snowstorm fluttered by; he saw the
   sun

Show and pass by, gleam from one towering
   prison
Into another, vaster and more grim,
Which in dull crags of darkness had arisen
To muffle-to a final door on him.
The gods upon the dull crags lowered dim,
The pigeons chattered, quarrelling in the
   track.
In the south-west the dimness dulled to
   black.

Then came the cry of "Call all hands on
   deck !"
The Dauber knew its meaning; it was
   come :
Cape Horn, that tramples beauty into wreck,

And crumples steel and smites the strong
    man dumb.

Down clattered flying kites and staysails:
    some

Sang out in quick, high calls: the fair-
    leads skirled,

And from the south-west came the end of
    the world.

"Caught in her ball-dress," said the Bosun,
    hauling;

"Lee-ay, lee-ay!" quick, high, came the
    men's call;

It was all wallop of sails and startled calling.

"Let fly!" "Let go!" "Clew up!" and
    "Let go all!"

"Now up and make them fast!" "Here,
    give us a haul!"

"Now up and stow them! Quick! By
    God! we're done!"

The blackness crunched all memory of the
    sun.

"Up!" said the Mate. "Mizen top-
    gallants. Hurry!"
The Dauber ran, the others ran, the sails
Slatted and shook; out of the black a
    flurry
Whirled in fine lines, tattering the edge
    to trails.
Painting and art and England were old
    tales
Told in some other life to that pale man,
Who struggled with white fear and gulped
    and ran.

He struck a ringbolt in his haste and fell —
Rose, sick with pain, half-lamed in his left
    knee;
He reached the shrouds where clambering
    men pell-mell

Hustled each other up and cursed him;
    he
Hurried aloft with them: then from the
    sea
Came a cold, sudden breath that made
    the hair
Stiff on the neck, as though Death whis-
    pered there.

A man below him punched him in the
    side.
"Get up, you Dauber, or let me get past."
He saw the belly of the skysail skied,
Gulped, and clutched tight, and tried to
    go more fast.
Sometimes he missed his ratline and was
    grassed,
Scraped his shin raw against the rigid line.
The clamberers reached the futtock-
    shrouds' incline.

Cursing they came; one, kicking out be-
    hind,

Kicked Dauber in the mouth, and one be-
    low

Punched at his calves; the futtock-shrouds
    inclined

It was a perilous path for one to go.

"Up, Dauber, up!" A curse followed a
    blow.

He reached the top and gasped, then on,
    then on.

And one voice yelled "Let go!" and one
    "All gone!"

Fierce clamberers, some in oilskins, some
    in rags,

Hustling and hurrying up, up the steep
    stairs.

Before the windless sails were blown to
    flags,

H

And whirled like dirty birds athwart great airs,

Ten men in all, to get this mast of theirs

Snugged to the gale in time. "Up! Damn
   you, run!"

The mizen topmast head was safely won.

"Lay out!" the Bosun yelled. The Dauber
   laid

Out on the yard, gripping the yard, and
   feeling

Sick at the mighty space of air displayed

Below his feet, where mewing birds were
   wheeling.

A giddy fear was on him; he was reeling.

He bit his lip half through, clutching the
   jack.

A cold sweat glued the shirt upon his
   back.

The yard was shaking, for a brace was
   loose.

He felt that he would fall; he clutched,
      he bent,
Clammy with natural terror to the shoes
While idiotic promptings came and went.
Snow fluttered on a wind-flaw and was
      spent;
He saw the water darken. Someone yelled,
"Frap it; don't stay to furl! Hold on!"
      He held.

Darkness came down — half darkness — in
      a whirl;
The sky went out, the waters disappeared.
He felt a shocking pressure of blowing hurl
The ship upon her side. The darkness
      speared
At her with wind; she staggered, she
      careered,
Then down she lay. The Dauber felt her
      go;

He saw his yard tilt downwards. Then
    the snow

Whirled all about — dense, multitudinous,
    cold —
Mixed with the wind's one devilish thrust
    and shriek,
Which whiffled out men's tears, deafened,
    took hold,
Flattening the flying drift against the
    cheek.
The yards buckled and bent, man could not
    speak.
The ship lay on her broadside; the wind's
    sound
Had devilish malice at having got her
    downed.

      *   *   *   *   *

How long the gale had blown he could not
    tell,

Only the world had changed, his life had
    died.

A moment now was everlasting hell.

Nature an onslaught from the weather
    side,

A withering rush of death, a frost that
    cried,

Shrieked, till he withered at the heart; a
    hail

Plastered his oilskins with an icy mail.

"Cut!" yelled his mate.   He looked — the
    sail was gone,

Blown into rags in the first furious squall;

The tatters drummed the devil's tattoo.
    On

The buckling yard a block thumped like
    a mall.

The ship lay — the sea smote her, the
    wind's bawl

Came, "loo, loo, loo!" The devil cried
    his hounds
On to the poor spent stag strayed in his
    bounds.

"Cut! Ease her!" yelled his mate; the
    Dauber heard.
His mate wormed up the tilted yard and
    slashed,
A rag of canvas skimmed like a darting bird.
The snow whirled, the ship bowed to it,
    the gear lashed,
The sea-tops were cut off and flung down
    smashed;
Tatters of shouts were flung, the rags of
    yells —
And clang, clang, clang, below beat the
    two bells.

"O God!" the Dauber moaned. A roar-
    ing rang,

Blasting the royals like a cannonade;

The backstays parted with a cracking clang,

The upper spars were snapped like twigs
  decayed —

Snapped at their heels, their jagged splin-
  ters splayed,

Like white and ghastly hair erect with fear.

The Mate yelled, "Gone, by God, and
  pitched them clear!"

"Up!" yelled the Bosun; "up and clear
  the wreck!"

The Dauber followed where he led: below

He caught one giddy glimpsing of the deck

Filled with white water, as though heaped
  with snow.

He saw the streamers of the rigging blow

Straight out like pennons from the splintered mast,

Then, all sense dimmed, all was an icy blast

Roaring from nether hell and filled with ice,

Roaring and crashing on the jerking stage,

An utter bridle given to utter vice,

Limitless power mad with endless rage

Withering the soul; a minute seemed an
    age.

He clutched and hacked at ropes, at rags
    of sail,

Thinking that comfort was a fairy-tale

Told long ago — long, long ago — long since

Heard of in other lives — imagined,
    dreamed —

There where the basest beggar was a prince

To him in torment where the tempest
    screamed,

Comfort and warmth and ease no longer
    seemed

Things that a man could know : soul, body,
    brain,

Knew nothing but the wind, the cold, the
    pain.

"Leave that!" the Bosun shouted; "Cro-
    jick save!"
The splitting crojick, not yet gone to rags,
Thundered below, beating till something
    gave,
Bellying between its buntlines into bags.
Some birds were blown past, shrieking:
    dark, like shags,
Their backs seemed, looking down. "Leu,
    leu!" they cried.
The ship lay, the seas thumped her; she
    had died.

They reached the crojick yard, which
    buckled, buckled
Like a thin whalebone to the topsail's
    strain.

They laid upon the yard and heaved and
    knuckled,
Pounding the sail, which jangled and leapt
    again.
It was quite hard with ice, its rope like
    chain,
Its strength like seven devils; it shook the
    mast.
They cursed and toiled and froze: a long
    time passed.

Two hours passed, then a dim lightening
    came.
Those frozen ones upon the yard could
    see
The mainsail and the foresail still the same,
Still battling with the hands and blowing
    free,
Rags tattered where the staysails used to
    be.

The lower topsails stood; the ship's lee
  deck
Seethed with four feet of water filled with
  wreck.

An hour more went by; the Dauber lost
All sense of hands and feet, all sense of all
But of a wind that cut him to the ghost,
And of a frozen fold he had to haul,
Of heavens that fell and never ceased to
  fall,
And ran in smoky snatches along the sea,
Leaping from crest to wave-crest, yelling.
  He

Lost sense of time; no bells went, but he
  felt
Ages go over him. At last, at last
They frapped the cringled crojick's icy pelt;
In frozen bulge and bunt they made it fast.

Then, scarcely live, they laid in to the mast.

The Captain's speaking trumpet gave a
     blare,

"Make fast the topsail, Mister, while you're
     there."

Some seamen cursed, but up they had to
     go —

Up to the topsail yard to spend an hour

Stowing a topsail in a blinding snow,

Which made the strongest man among them
     cower.

More men came up, the fresh hands gave
     them power,

They stowed the sail; then with a rattle
     of chain

One half the crojick burst its bonds again.

    *   *   *   *   *

They stowed the sail, frapping it round with
     rope,

Leaving no surface for the wind, no fold,

Then down the weather shrouds, half dead,
> they grope;

That struggle with the sail had made them
> old.

They wondered if the crojick furl would
> hold.

"Lucky," said one, "it didn't spring the
> spar."

"Lucky!" the Bosun said, "Lucky! We
> are!

She came within two shakes of turning
> top

Or stripping all her shroud-screws, that
> first quiff.

Now fish those wash-deck buckets out of
> the slop.

Here's Dauber says he doesn't like Cape
> Stiff.

This isn't wind, man, this is only a whiff.

Hold on, all hands, hold on!" a sea, half
 seen,

Paused, mounted, burst, and filled the
 main-deck green.

The Dauber felt a mountain of water fall.

It covered him deep, deep, he felt it fill,

Over his head, the deck, the fife-rails, all,

Quieting the ship, she trembled and lay
 still.

Then with a rush and shatter and clanging shrill

Over she went; he saw the water cream

Over the bitts; he saw the half-deck
 stream.

Then in the rush he swirled, over she went;

Her lee-rail dipped, he struck, and something gave;

His legs went through a port as the roll
      spent;
She paused, then rolled, and back the water
      drave.
He drifted with it as a part of the wave,
Drowning, half-stunned, exhausted, partly
      frozen,
He struck the booby hatchway; then the
      Bosun

Leaped, seeing his chance, before the next
      sea burst,
And caught him as he drifted, seized him,
      held,
Up-ended him against the bitts, and cursed.
"This ain't the George's Swimming Baths,"
      he yelled;
"Keep on your feet!" Another grey-back
      felled
The two together, and the Bose, half-blind,

Spat: "One's a joke," he cursed, "but
    two's unkind."

"Now, damn it, Dauber!" said the Mate.
    "Look out,
Or you'll be over the side!" The water
    freed;
Each clanging freeing-port became a spout.
The men cleared up the decks as there was
    need.
The Dauber's head was cut, he felt it bleed
Into his oilskins as he clutched and coiled.
Water and sky were devils' brews which
    boiled,

Boiled, shrieked, and glowered; but the
    ship was saved.
Snugged safely down, though fourteen sails
    were split.
Out of the dark a fiercer fury raved.

The grey-backs died and mounted, each
    crest lit

With a white toppling gleam that hissed
    from it

And slid, or leaped, or ran with whirls of
    cloud,

Mad with inhuman life that shrieked aloud.

The watch was called; Dauber might go
    below.

"Splice the main brace!" the Mate called.
    All laid aft

To get a gulp of momentary glow

As some reward for having saved the
    craft.

The steward ladled mugs, from which each
    quaff'd

Whisky, with water, sugar, and lime-juice,
    hot,

A quarter of a pint each made the tot.

I

Beside the lamp-room door the steward
    stood
Ladling it out, and each man came in turn,
Tipped his sou'-wester, drank it, grunted
    "Good!"
And shambled forward, letting it slowly
    burn:
When all were gone the Dauber lagged
    astern,
Torn by his frozen body's lust for heat,
The liquor's pleasant smell, so warm, so
    sweet,

And by a promise long since made at home
Never to taste strong liquor. Now he
    knew
The worth of liquor; now he wanted
    some.
His frozen body urged him to the brew;
Yet it seemed wrong, an evil thing to do

To break that promise. "Dauber," said
    the Mate,

"Drink, and turn in, man; why the hell
    d'ye wait?"

"Please, sir, I'm temperance." "Temper-
    ance are you, hey?

That's all the more for me! So you're
    for slops?

I thought you'd had enough slops for to-
    day.

Go to your bunk and ease her when she
    drops.

And — damme, steward! you brew with
    too much hops!

Stir up the sugar, man! — and tell your girl

How kind the Mate was teaching you to
    furl."

Then the Mate drank the remnants, six
    men's share,

And ramped into his cabin, where he
    stripped
And danced unclad, and was uproarious
    there.
In waltzes with the cabin cat he tripped,
Singing in tenor clear that he was pipped —
That "he who strove the tempest to dis-
    arm,
Must never first embrail the lee yard-
    arm,"

And that his name was Ginger. Dauber
    crept
Back to the round-house, gripping by the
    rail.
The wind howled by; the passionate water
    leapt;
The night was all one roaring with the gale.
Then at the door he stopped, uttering a
    wail;

His hands were perished numb and blue as
      veins,
He could not turn the knob for both the
      Spains.

A hand came shuffling aft, dodging the seas,
Singing "her nut-brown hair" between his
      teeth ;
Taking the ocean's tumult at his ease
Even when the wash about his thighs did
      seethe.
His soul was happy in its happy sheath ;
"What, Dauber, won't it open? Fingers
      cold?
You'll talk of this time, Dauber, when
      you're old."

He flung the door half open, and a sea
Washed them both in, over the splash-
      board, down ;

"You silly, salt miscarriage!" sputtered
 he.

"Dauber, pull out the plug before we
 drown!

That's spoiled my laces and my velvet
 gown.

Where is the plug?" Groping in pitch
 dark water,

He sang between his teeth "The Farmer's
 Daughter."

It was pitch dark within there; at each roll

The chests slid to the slant; the water
 rushed,

Making full many a clanging tin pan bowl

Into the black below-bunks as it gushed.

The dog-tired men slept through it; they
 were hushed.

The water drained, and then with matches
 damp

The man struck heads off till he lit the lamp.

"Thank you," the Dauber said; the sea-
    man grinned.
"This is your first foul weather?" "Yes."
    "I thought
Up on the yard you hadn't seen much wind.
Them's rotten sea-boots, Dauber, that you
    brought.
Now I must cut on deck before I'm
    caught."
He went; the lamp-flame smoked; he
    slammed the door;
A film of water loitered across the floor.

The Dauber watched it come and watched
    it go;
He had had revelation of the lies
Cloaking the truth men never choose to
    know;

He could bear witness now and cleanse
their eyes.
He had beheld in suffering; he was wise;
This was the sea, this searcher of the soul —
This never-dying shriek fresh from the
Pole.

He shook with cold; his hands could not
undo
His oilskin buttons, so he shook and sat,
Watching his dirty fingers, dirty blue,
Hearing without the hammering tackle slat,
Within, the drops from dripping clothes
went pat,
Running in little patters, gentle, sweet,
And "Ai, ai!" went the wind, and the
seas beat.

His bunk was sopping wet; he clambered
in.

None of his clothes were dry; his fear
    recurred.
Cramps bunched the muscles underneath
    his skin.
The great ship rolled until the lamp was
    blurred.
He took his Bible and tried to read a word;
Trembled at going aloft again, and then
Resolved to fight it out and show it to
    men.

Faces recurred, fierce memories of the yard,
The frozen sail, the savage eyes, the jests,
The oaths of one great seaman, syphilis-
    scarred,
The tug of leeches jammed beneath their
    chests,
The buntlines bellying bunts out into
    breasts.
The deck so desolate-grey, the sky so wild,

He fell asleep, and slept like a young
　　child.

But not for long; the cold awoke him
　　soon,
The hot-ache and the skin-cracks and the
　　cramp,
The seas thundering without, the gale's
　　wild tune,
The sopping misery of the blankets damp.
A speaking-trumpet roared; a sea-boot's
　　stamp
Clogged at the door. A man entered to
　　shout:
"All hands on deck! Arouse here! Tum-
　　ble out!"

The caller raised the lamp; his oilskins
　　clicked
As the thin ice upon them cracked and
　　fell.

"Rouse out!" he said. "This lamp is
frozen wick'd.

Rouse out!" His accent deepened to a
yell.

"We're among ice; it's blowing up like
hell.

We're going to hand both topsails. Time,
I guess,

We're sheeted up. Rouse out! Don't
stay to dress!"

"Is it cold on deck?" said Dauber. "Is
it cold?

We're sheeted up, I tell you, inches thick!

The fo'c'sle's like a wedding-cake, I'm
told.

Now tumble out, my sons; on deck here,
quick!

Rouse out, away, and come and climb the
stick.

I'm going to call the half-deck. Bosun!
  Hey!
Both topsails coming in. Heave out!
  Away!"

He went; the Dauber tumbled from his
  bunk,
Clutching the side. He heard the wind go
  past,
Making the great ship wallow as if drunk.
There was a shocking tumult up the mast.
"This is the end," he muttered, "come at
  last!
I've got to go aloft, facing this cold.
I can't. I can't. I'll never keep my hold.

"I cannot face the topsail yard again.
I never guessed what misery it would be."
The cramps and hot-ache made him sick
  with pain.

The ship stopped suddenly from a devilish
   sea,
Then, with a triumph of wash, a rush of
   glee,
The door burst in, and in the water rolled,
Filling the lower bunks, black, creaming,
   cold.

The lamp sucked out.   "Wash!" went
   the water back,
Then in again, flooding; the Bosun swore.
"You useless thing! You Dauber! You
   lee slack!
Get out, you heekapoota! Shut the door!
You coo-ilyaira, what are you waiting
   for?
Out of my way, you thing — you useless
   thing!"
He slammed the door indignant, clanging
   the ring.

And then he lit the lamp, drowned to the
    waist;

"Here's a fine house! Get at the scupper-
    holes" —

He bent against it as the water raced —

"And pull them out to leeward when she
    rolls.

They say some kinds of landsmen don't
    have souls.

I well believe. A Port Mahon baboon

Would make more soul than you got with
    a spoon."

Down in the icy water Dauber groped

To find the plug; the racing water sluiced

Over his head and shoulders as she sloped.

Without, judged by the sound, all hell was
    loosed.

He felt cold Death about him tightly
    noosed.

That Death was better than the misery
    there
Iced on the quaking foothold high in air.

And then the thought came: "I'm a failure.
    All
My life has been a failure.   They were
    right.
It will not matter if I go and fall;
I should be free then from this hell's de-
    light.
I'll never paint.   Best let it end to-night.
I'll slip over the side.   I've tried and
    failed."
So in the ice-cold in the night he quailed.

Death would be better, death, than this
    long hell
Of mockery and surrender and dismay —
This long defeat of doing nothing well,

Playing the part too high for him to
play.

"O Death ! who hides the sorry thing away,

Take me ; I've failed. I cannot play these
cards."

There came a thundering from the topsail
yards.

And then he bit his lips, clenching his
mind,

And staggered out to muster, beating back

The coward frozen self of him that whined.

Come what cards might he meant to play
the pack.

"Ai !" screamed the wind ; the topsail
sheet went clack ;

Ice filled the air with spikes ; the grey-
backs burst.

"Here's Dauber," said the Mate, "on deck
the first.

"Why, holy sailor, Dauber, you're a man!
I took you for a soldier.   Up now, come!"
Up on the yards already they began
That battle with a gale which strikes men
    dumb.
The leaping topsail thundered like a drum.
The frozen snow beat in the face like shots.
The wind spun whipping wave-crests into
    clots.

So up upon the topsail yard again,
In the great tempest's fiercest hour, began
Probation to the Dauber's soul, of pain
Which crowds a century's torment in a span.
For the next month the ocean taught this
    man,
And he, in that month's torment, while
    she wested,
Was never warm nor dry, nor full nor
    rested.

K

But still it blew, or, if it lulled, it rose
Within the hour and blew again; and still
The water as it burst aboard her froze.
The wind blew off an ice-field, raw and chill,
Daunting man's body, tampering with his
    will;
But after thirty days a ghostly sun
Gave sickly promise that the storms were
    done.

VII

A GREAT grey sea was running up the sky,
Desolate birds flew past; their mewings
    came
As that lone water's spiritual cry,
Its forlorn voice, its essence, its soul's name.
The ship limped in the water as if lame.
Then in the forenoon watch to a great
    shout

More sail was made, the reefs were shaken
    out.

A slant came from the south; the singers
    stood
Clapped to the halliards, hauling to a tune,
Old as the sea, a fillip to the blood.
The upper topsail rose like a balloon.
"So long, Cape Stiff. In Valparaiso
    soon,"
Said one to other, as the ship lay over,
Making her course again — again a rover.

Slowly the sea went down as the wind
    fell.
Clear rang the songs, "Hurrah ! Cape Horn
    is bet !"
The combless seas were lumping into swell;
The leaking fo'c'sles were no longer wet.
More sail was made; the watch on deck
    was set

To cleaning up the ruin broken bare
Below, aloft, about her, everywhere.

The Dauber, scrubbing out the round-
    house, found
Old pantiles pulped among the mouldy
    gear,
Washed underneath the bunks and long
    since drowned
During the agony of the Cape Horn year.
He sang in scrubbing, for he had done with
    fear —
Fronted the worst and looked it in the
    face;
He had got manhood at the testing-place.

Singing he scrubbed, passing his watch
    below,
Making the round-house fair; the Bosun
    watched,

Bringing his knitting slowly to the toe.

Sails stretched a mizen skysail which he
    patched;

They thought the Dauber was a bad egg
    hatched.

"Daubs," said the Bosun cheerly, "can you
    knit?

I've made a Barney's bull of this last
    bit."

Then, while the Dauber counted, Bosun
    took

Some marline from his pocket. "Here,"
    he said,

"You want to know square sennit? So
    fash. Look!

Eight foxes take, and stop the ends with
    thread.

I've known an engineer would give his
    head

To know square sennit." As the Bose
    began,
The Dauber felt promoted into man.

It was his warrant that he had not failed —
That the most hard part in his difficult
    climb
Had not been past attainment; it was
    scaled:
Safe footing showed above the slippery
    slime.
He had emerged out of the iron time,
And knew that he could compass his life's
    scheme;
He had the power sufficient to his dream.

Then dinner came, and now the sky was
    blue.
The ship was standing north, the Horn was
    rounded;

She made a thundering as she weltered
    through.

The mighty grey-backs glittered as she
    bounded.

More sail was piled upon her; she was
    hounded

North, while the wind came; like a stag
    she ran

Over grey hills and hollows of seas wan.

She had a white bone in her mouth: she
    sped;

Those in the round-house watched her as
    they ate

Their meal of pork-fat fried with broken
    bread.

"Good old!" they cried. "She's off; she's
    gathering gait!"

Her track was whitening like a Lammas
    spate.

"Good old!" they cried. "Oh, give her
　　　cloth! Hurray!
For three weeks more to Valparaiso Bay!

"She smells old Vallipo," the Bosun cried.
"We'll be inside the tier in three weeks
　　　more,
Lying at double-moorings where they ride
Off of the market, half a mile from shore,
And bumboat pan, my sons, and figs galore,
And girls in black mantillas fit to make a
Poor seaman frantic when they dance the
　　　cueca."

Eight bells were made, the watch was
　　　changed, and now
The Mate spoke to the Dauber: "This is
　　　better.
We'll soon be getting mudhooks over the
　　　bow.

She'll make her passage still if this'll let
    her.
Oh, run, you drogher! dip your fo'c'sle
    wetter.
Well, Dauber, this is better than Cape
    Horn.
Them topsails made you wish you'd not
    been born."

"Yes, sir," the Dauber said. "Now," said
    the Mate,
"We've got to smart her up. Them Cape
    Horn seas
Have made her paint-work like a rusty grate.
Oh, didn't them topsails make your fish-
    hooks freeze?
A topsail don't pay heed to 'Won't you,
    please?'
Well, you have seen Cape Horn, my son;
    you've learned.

You've dipped your hand and had your
      fingers burned.

"And now you'll stow that folly, trying
      to paint.
You've had your lesson; you're a sailor
      now.
You come on board a female ripe to faint.
All sorts of slush you'd learned, the Lord
      knows how.
Cape Horn has sent you wisdom over the
      bow
If you've got sense to take it. You're a
      sailor.
My God! before you were a woman's tailor.

"So throw your paints to blazes and have
      done.
Words can't describe the silly things you
      did

Sitting before your easel in the sun,

With all your colours on the paint-box
    lid.

I blushed for you . . . and then the daubs
    you hid.

My God! you'll have more sense now, eh?
    You've quit?"

"No, sir." "You've not?" "No, sir."
    "God give you wit.

"I thought you'd come to wisdom." Thus
    they talked,

While the great clipper took her bit and
    rushed

Like a skin-glistening stallion not yet
    baulked,

Till fire-bright water at her swing ports
    gushed;

Poising and bowing down her fore-foot
    crushed

Bubble on glittering bubble; on she went.
The Dauber watched her, wondering what
          it meant.

To come, after long months, at rosy dawn,
Into the placid blue of some great bay.
Treading the quiet water like a fawn
Ere yet the morning haze was blown away.
A rose-flushed figure putting by the grey,
And anchoring there before the city smoke
Rose, or the church-bells rang, or men
          awoke.

And then, in the first light, to see grow
          clear
That long-expected haven filled with
          strangers —
Alive with men and women; see and hear
Its clattering market and its money-
          changers;

And hear the surf beat, and be free from
    dangers,
And watch the crinkled ocean blue with
    calm
Drowsing beneath the Trade, beneath the
    palm.

Hungry for that he worked; the hour
    went by,
And still the wind grew, still the clipper
    strode,
And now a darkness hid the western
    sky,
And sprays came flicking off at the wind's
    goad.
She stumbled now, feeling her sail a load.
The Mate gazed hard to windward, eyed
    his sail,
And said the Horn was going to flick her
    tail.

Boldly he kept it on her till she staggered,

But still the wind increased; it grew, it
grew,

Darkening the sky, making the water hag-
gard;

Full of small snow the mighty wester blew.

"More fun for little fish-hooks," sighed
the crew.

They eyed the taut topgallants stiff like
steel;

A second hand was ordered to the wheel.

The Captain eyed her aft, sucking his lip,

Feeling the sail too much, but yet refrain-
ing

From putting hobbles on the leaping ship,

The glad sea-shattering stallion, halter-
straining,

Wing-musical, uproarious, and complaining;

But, in a gust, he cocked his finger, so:
"You'd better take them off, before they
    go."

All saw. They ran at once without the
    word
"Lee-ay! Lee-ay!" Loud rang the clew-
    line cries;
Sam in his bunk within the half-deck heard,
Stirred in his sleep, and rubbed his drowsy
    eyes.
"There go the lower to'gallants." Against
    the skies
Rose the thin bellying strips of leaping
    sail.
The Dauber was the first man over the
    rail.

Three to a mast they ran; it was a race.
"God!" said the Mate; "that Dauber,
    he can go."

He watched the runners with an upturned
    face
Over the futtocks, struggling heel to toe,
Up to the topmast cross-trees into the
    blow
Where the three sails were leaping.
    "Dauber wins!"
The yards were reached, and now the race
    begins.

Which three will furl their sail first and
    come down?
Out to the yard-arm for the leech goes one,
His hair blown flagwise from a hatless
    crown,
His hands at work like fever to be done.
Out of the gale a fiercer fury spun.
The three sails leaped together, yanking
    high,
Like talons darting up to clutch the sky.

The Dauber on the fore-topgallant yard
Out at the weather yard-arm was the first
To lay his hand upon the buntline-barred
Topgallant yanking to the wester's burst;
He craned to catch the leech; his comrades
cursed;
One at the buntlines, one with oaths
observed,
"The eye of the outer jib-stay isn't
served."

"No," said the Dauber. "No," the man
replied.
They heaved, stowing the sail, not looking
round,
Panting, but full of life and eager-eyed;
The gale roared at them with its iron
sound.
"That's you," the Dauber said. His gasket wound

L

Swift round the yard, binding the sail in
    bands;

There came a gust, the sail leaped from his
    hands,

So that he saw it high above him, grey,

And there his mate was falling; quick he
    clutched

An arm in oilskins swiftly snatched away.

A voice said "Christ!" a quick shape
    stooped and touched,

Chain struck his hands, ropes shot, the sky
    was smutched

With vast black fires that ran, that fell,
    that furled,

And then he saw the mast, the small snow
    hurled,

The fore-topgallant yard far, far aloft,

And blankness settling on him and great
    pain;

And snow beneath his fingers wet and soft,

And topsail sheet-blocks shaking at the
   chain.

He knew it was he who had fallen; then his
   brain

Swirled in a circle while he watched the sky.

Infinite multitudes of snow blew by.

"I thought it was Tom who fell," his brain's
   voice said.

"Down on the bloody deck!" the Captain screamed.

The multitudinous little snow-flakes sped.

His pain was real enough, but all else
   seemed.

Si with a bucket ran, the water gleamed

Tilting upon him; others came, the
   Mate . . .

They knelt with eager eyes like things that
   wait

For other things to come. He saw them
    there.

"It will go on," he murmured, watching Si.

Colours and sounds seemed mixing in the
    air,

The pain was stunning him, and the wind
    went by.

"More water," said the Mate. "Here,
    Bosun, try.

Ask if he's got a message. Hell, he's gone!

Here, Dauber, paints." He said, "It will
    go on."

Not knowing his meaning rightly, but he
    spoke

With the intenseness of a fading soul

Whose share of Nature's fire turns to smoke,

Whose hand on Nature's wheel loses
    control.

The eager faces glowered red like coal.

They glowed, the great storm glowed, the
    sails, the mast.

"It will go on," he cried aloud, and passed.

Those from the yard came down to tell
    the tale.

"He almost had me off," said Tom. "He
    slipped.

There come one hell of a jump-like from
    the sail. . . .

He clutched at me and almost had me
    pipped.

He caught my 'ris'band, but the oilskin
    ripped. . . .

It tore clean off. Look here. I was near
    gone.

I made a grab to catch him; so did John.

"I caught his arm. My God! I was near
    done.

He almost had me over; it was near.

He hit the ropes and grabbed at every one."

"Well," said the Mate, "we cannot leave
him here.

Run, Si, and get the half-deck table clear.

We'll lay him there. Catch hold there,
you, and you,

He's dead, poor son; there's nothing more
to do."

Night fell, and all night long the Dauber
lay

Covered upon the table; all night long

The pitiless storm exulted at her prey,

Huddling the waters with her icy thong.

But to the covered shape she did no wrong.

He lay beneath the sailcloth. Bell by
bell

The night wore through; the stars rose,
the stars fell.

Blowing most pitiless cold out of clear sky
The wind roared all night long; and all
    night through
The green seas on the deck went washing by,
Flooding the half-deck; bitter hard it blew.
But little of it all the Dauber knew —
The sopping bunks, the floating chests,
    the wet,
The darkness, and the misery, and the
    sweat.

He was off duty. So it blew all night,
And when the watches changed the men
    would come
Dripping within the door to strike a light
And stare upon the Dauber lying dumb,
And say, "He come a cruel thump, poor
    chum."
Or, "He'd a-been a fine big man;" or,
    "He . . .

A smart young seaman he was getting to
be."

Or, "Damn it all, it's what we've all to
face ! . .
I knew another fellow one time . . ." then
Came a strange tale of death in a strange
place
Out on the sea, in ships, with wandering
men.
In many ways Death puts us into pen.
The reefers came down tired and looked
and slept.
Below the skylight little dribbles crept

Along the painted woodwork, glistening,
slow,
Following the roll and dripping, never fast,
But dripping on the quiet form below,
Like passing time talking to time long past.

And all night long "Ai, ai!" went the wind's
    blast,
And creaming water swished below the
    pale,
Unheeding body stretched beneath the sail.

At dawn they sewed him up, and at eight
    bells
They bore him to the gangway, wading
    deep,
Through the green-clutching, white-toothed
    water-hells
That flung his carriers over in their sweep.
They laid an old red ensign on the heap,
And all hands stood bare-headed, stooping,
    swaying,
Washed by the sea while the old man was
    praying

Out of a borrowed prayer-book. At a sign

They twitched the ensign back and tipped
the grating

A creamier bubbling broke the bubbling
brine.

The muffled figure tilted to the weight-
ing;

It dwindled slowly down, slowly gyrating.

Some craned to see; it dimmed, it disappeared;

The last green milky bubble blinked and
cleared.

"Mister, shake out your reefs," the Captain called.

"Out topsail reefs!" the Mate cried; then
all hands

Hurried, the great sails shook, and all hands
hauled,

Singing that desolate song of lonely lands,

Of how a lover came in dripping bands,

Green with the wet and cold, to tell his
    lover
That Death was in the sea, and all was
    over.

Fair came the falling wind; a seaman said
The Dauber was a Jonah; once again
The clipper held her course, showing red
    lead,
Shattering the sea-tops into golden rain.
The waves bowed down before her like
    blown grain;
Onwards she thundered, on; her voyage
    was short,
Before the tier's bells rang her into port.

Cheerly they rang her in, those beating
    bells,
The new-come beauty stately from the sea,
Whitening the blue heave of the drowsy
    swells,

Treading the bubbles down. With three
  times three
They cheered her moving beauty in, and
  she
Came to her berth so noble, so superb;
Swayed like a queen, and answered to the
  curb.

Then in the sunset's flush they went aloft,
And unbent sails in that most lovely hour,
When the light gentles and the wind is soft,
And beauty in the heart breaks like a flower.
Working aloft they saw the mountain
  tower,
Snow to the peak; they heard the launch-
  men shout;
And bright along the bay the lights came
  out.

And then the night fell dark, and all night
  long

The pointed mountain pointed at the stars,

Frozen, alert, austere; the eagle's song

Screamed from her desolate screes and
  splintered scars.

On her intense crags where the air is sparse

The stars looked down; their many golden
  eyes

Watched her and burned, burned out, and
  came to rise.

Silent the finger of the summit stood,

Icy in pure, thin air, glittering with snows.

Then the sun's coming turned the peak to
  blood,

And in the rest-house the muleteers arose.

And all day long, where only the eagle
  goes,

Stones, loosened by the sun, fall; the stones
  falling

Fill empty gorge on gorge with echoes calling.

EXPLANATIONS OF SOME OF THE SEA TERMS USED IN THE POEM

Backstays. Wire ropes which support the masts against lateral and after strains.

Barney's bull. A figure in marine proverb. A jewel in marine repartee.

Bells. Two bells (one forward, one aft) which are struck every half-hour in a certain manner to mark the passage of the watches.

Bitts. Strong wooden structures (built round each mast) upon which running rigging is secured.

Block. A sheaved pulley.

Boatswain. A supernumerary or idler, generally attached to the mate's watch, and holding considerable authority over the crew.

Bouilli tin. Any tin that contains, or has contained, preserved meat.

Bows. The forward extremity of a ship.

Brace-blocks. Pulleys through which the braces travel.

Braces. Ropes by which the yards are inclined forward or aft.

Bumboat pan. Soft bread sold by the bumboat man, a kind of sea costermonger who trades with ships in port.

Bunt. Those cloths of a square sail which are nearest to the mast when the sail is set. The central portion of a furled square sail. The human abdomen (figuratively).

Buntlines. Ropes which help to confine square sails to the yards in the operation of furling.

Chocks. Wooden stands on which the boats rest.

Cleats. Iron or wooden contrivances to which ropes may be secured.

Clew-lines. Ropes by which the lower corners of square sails are lifted.

Clews. The lower corners of square sails.

Clipper. A title of honour given to ships of more than usual speed and beauty.

Coaming. The raised rim of a hatchway; a barrier at a doorway to keep water from entering.

Courses. The large square sails set upon the lower yards of sailing ships. The mizen course is called the " crojick."

Cringled. Fitted with iron rings or cringles, many of which are let into sails or sail-roping for various purposes.

Crojick (or cross-jack). A square sail set upon the lower yard of the mizen mast.

Dungarees. Thin blue or khaki-coloured overalls made from cocoanut fibre.

Fairleads. Rings of wood or iron by means of which running rigging is led in any direction.

Fife-rails. Strong wooden shelves fitted with iron pins, to which ropes may be secured.

Fish-hooks. *I.e.*, fingers.

Foot-ropes. Ropes on which men stand when working aloft.

Fo'c'sle. The cabin or cabins in which the men are berthed. It is usually an iron deck-house divided through the middle into two compartments for the two watches, and fitted with wooden bunks.

Sometimes it is even fitted with lockers and an iron water-tank.

Foxes. Strands, yarns, or arrangements of yarns of rope.

Freeing-ports. Iron doors in the ship's side which open outwards to free the decks of water.

Frap. To wrap round with rope.

Futtock-shrouds. Iron bars to which the topmast rigging is secured. As they project outward and upward from the masts they are difficult to clamber over.

Galley. The ship's kitchen.

Gantline (girtline). A rope used for the sending of sails up and down from aloft.

Gaskets. Ropes by which the sails are secured in furling.

Half-deck. A cabin or apartment in which the apprentices are berthed. Its situation is usually the ship's waist; but it is sometimes further aft, and occasionally it is under the poop or even right forward under the top-gallant fo'c'sle.

Halliards. Ropes by which sails are hoisted.

Harness-room. An office or room from which the salt meat is issued, and in which it is sometimes stored.

Hawse. The bows or forward end of a ship.

Head. The forward part of a ship. That upper edge of a square sail which is attached to the yard.

House-flag. The special flag of the firm to which a ship belongs.

Idlers. The members of the round-house mess, generally consisting of the carpenter, cook, sailmaker, boatswain, painter, etc., are known as the idlers.

Jack (or jackstay). An iron bar (fitted along all yards in sailing ships) to which the head of a square sail is secured when bent.

Kites. Light upper sails.

Leeches. The outer edges of square sails. In furling some square sails the leech is dragged inwards till it lies level with the head upon the surface of the yard. This is done by the first man who gets upon the yard, beginning at the weather side.

Logship. A contrivance by which a ship's speed is measured.

Lower topsail. The second sail from the deck on square rigged masts. It is a very strong, important sail.

Marline. Tarry line or coarse string made of rope-yarns twisted together.

Mate. The First or Chief Mate is generally called the Mate.

Mizen-topmast-head. The summit of the second of the three or four spars which make the complete mizen-mast.

Mudhooks. Anchors.

Pins. Iron or wooden bars to which running rigging is secured.

Pointing. A kind of neat plait with which ropes are sometimes ended off or decorated.

Poop-break. The forward end of the after superstructure.

Ratlines. The rope steps placed across the shrouds to enable the seamen to go aloft.

Reefers. Apprentices.

Reef-points. Ropes by which the area of some sails may be reduced in the operation of reefing. Reef-points are securely fixed to the sails fitted with

M

them, and when not in use their ends patter con-
tinually upon the canvas with a gentle drumming
noise.

Reel. A part of the machinery used with a logship.

Round-house. A cabin (of all shapes except round)
in which the idlers are berthed.

Royals. Light upper square sails; the fourth, fifth,
or sixth sails from the deck according to the mast's
rig.

Sail-room. A large room or compartment in which
the ship's sails are stored.

" Sails." The sailmaker is meant.

Scuttle-butt. A cask containing fresh water.

Shackles. Rope handles for a sea-chest.

Sheet-blocks. Iron blocks, by means of which sails
are sheeted home. In any violent wind they beat
upon the mast with great rapidity and force.

Sheets. Ropes or chains which extend the lower
corners of square sails in the operation of sheeting
home.

Shifting suits (of sails). The operation of removing
a ship's sails, and replacing them with others.

Shrouds. Wire ropes of great strength, which support
lateral strains on masts.

Shroud-screws. Iron contrivances by which shrouds
are hove taut.

Sidelights. A sailing ship carries two of these between
sunset and sunrise: one green, to starboard; one
red, to port.

Sights. Observations to help in the finding of a ship's
position.

Skid. A wooden contrivance on which ship's boats
rest.

Skysails. The uppermost square sails; the fifth, sixth, or seventh sails from the deck according to the mast's rig.

Slatting. The noise made by sails flogging in the wind.

Slush. Grease, melted fat.

South-wester. A kind of oilskin hat. A gale from the south-west.

Spit brown. To chew tobacco.

Square sennit. A cunning plait which makes a four-square bar.

Staysails. Fore and aft sails set upon the stays between the masts.

Stow. To furl.

Strop (the, putting on). A strop is a grument or rope ring. The two players kneel down facing each other, the strop is placed over their heads, and the men then try to pull each other over by the strength of their neck-muscles.

Swing ports. Iron doors in the ship's side which open outwards to free the decks from water.

Tackle (pronounced "taykel"). Blocks, ropes, pulleys, etc.

Take a caulk. To sleep upon the deck.

Topsails. The second and third sails from the deck on the masts of a modern square-rigged ship are known as the lower and upper topsails.

Trucks. The summits of the masts.

Upper topsail. The third square sail from the deck on the masts of square-rigged ships.

Yards. The steel or wooden spars (placed across masts) from which square sails are set.

BIOGRAPHY

WHEN I am buried, all my thoughts and acts
Will be reduced to lists of dates and facts,
And long before this wandering flesh is
　　rotten
The dates which made me will be all for-
　　gotten;
And none will know the gleam there used
　　to be
About the feast days freshly kept by me,
But men will call the golden hour of bliss
"About this time," or "shortly after this."

Men do not heed the rungs by which men
　　climb
Those glittering steps, those milestones upon
　　Time,

Those tombstones of dead selves, those
  hours of birth,
Those moments of the soul in years of earth
They mark the height achieved, the main
  result,
The power of freedom in the perished cult,
The power of boredom in the dead man's
  deeds,
Not the bright moments of the sprinkled
  seeds.

By many waters and on many ways
I have known golden instants and bright
  days;
The day on which, beneath an arching sail,
I saw the Cordilleras and gave hail;
The summer day on which in heart's delight
I saw the Swansea Mumbles bursting white,
The glittering day when all the waves wore
  flags

And the ship *Wanderer* came with sails in
rags;
That curlew-calling time in Irish dusk
When life became more splendid than its
husk,
When the rent chapel on the brae at Slains
Shone with a doorway opening beyond
brains;
The dawn when, with a brace-block's creak-
ing cry,
Out of the mist a little barque slipped by,
Spilling the mist with changing gleams of
red,
Then gone, with one raised hand and one
turned head;
The howling evening when the spindrift's
mists
Broke to display the four Evangelists,
Snow-capped, divinely granite, lashed by
breakers,

Wind-beaten bones of long since buried
    acres;

The night alone near water when I heard

All the sea's spirit spoken by a bird;

The English dusk when I beheld once more

(With eyes so changed) the ship, the citied
    shore,

The lines of masts, the streets so cheerly
    trod

(In happier seasons) and gave thanks to
    God.

All had their beauty, their bright moments'
    gift,

Their something caught from Time, the
    ever-swift.

All of those gleams were golden; but life's
    hands

Have given more constant gifts in changing
    lands,

And when I count those gifts, I think them
such

As no man's bounty could have bettered
much:

The gift of country life, near hills and
woods

Where happy waters sing in solitudes,

The gift of being near ships, of seeing each
day

A city of ships with great ships under
weigh,

The great street paved with water, filled
with shipping,

And all the world's flags flying and seagulls
dipping.

Yet when I am dust my penman may not
know

Those water-trampling ships which made
me glow,

But think my wonder mad and fail to
    find
Their glory, even dimly, from my mind,
And yet they made me :

                  not alone the ships
But men hard-palmed from tallying-on to
    whips,
The two close friends of nearly twenty
    years,
Sea-followers both, sea-wrestlers and sea-
    peers,
Whose feet with mine wore many a bolt-
    head bright
Treading the decks beneath the riding light.
Yet death will make that warmth of friend-
    ship cold
And who'll know what one said and what
    one told
Our hearts' communion and the broken
    spells

When the loud call blew at the strike of
     bells ?
No one, I know, yet let me be believed
A soul entirely known is life achieved.

Years blank with hardship never speak a
     word
Live in the soul to make the being stirred,
Towns can be prisons where the spirit dulls
Away from mates and ocean-wandering hulls,
Away from all bright water and great hills
And sheep-walks where the curlews cry their
     fills,
Away in towns, where eyes have nought to
     see
But dead museums and miles of misery
And floating life unrooted from man's need
And miles of fish-hooks baited to catch
     greed
And life made wretched out of human ken

And miles of shopping women served by men.

So, if the penman sums my London days

Let him but say that there were holy ways,

Dull Bloomsbury streets of dull brick man-
    sions old

With stinking doors where women stood to
    scold

And drunken waits at Christmas with their
    horn

Droning the news, in snow, that Christ was
    born;

And windy gas lamps and the wet roads
    shining

And that old carol of the midnight whining,

And that old room (above the noisy slum)

Where there was wine and fire and talk
    with some

Under strange pictures of the wakened soul

To whom this earth was but a burnt-out
    coal.

O Time, bring back those midnights and
    those friends,
Those glittering moments that a spirit lends
That all may be imagined from the flash
The cloud-hid god-game through the light-
    ning gash
Those hours of stricken sparks from which
    men took
Light to send out to men in song or
    book.
Those friends who heard St. Pancras' bells
    strike two
Yet stayed until the barber's cockerel crew.
Talking of noble styles, the Frenchman's
    best,
The thought beyond great poets not ex-
    pressed,
The glory of mood where human frailty
    failed,
The forts of human light not yet assailed,

Till the dim room had mind and seemed to
    brood
Binding our wills to mental brotherhood,
Till we became a college, and each night
Was discipline and manhood and delight,
Till our farewells and winding down the
    stairs
At each grey dawn had meaning that Time
    spares,
That we, so linked, should roam the whole
    world round
Teaching the ways our brooding minds had
    found
Making that room our Chapter, our one
    mind
Where all that this world soiled should be
    refined.

Often at night I tread those streets again
And see the alley glimmering in the rain,

Yet now I miss that sign of earlier tramps
A house with shadows of plane-boughs under
    lamps,
The secret house where once a beggar stood
Trembling and blind to show his woe for
    food.
And now I miss that friend who used to
    walk
Home to my lodgings with me, deep in
    talk,
Wearing the last of night out in still
    streets
Trodden by us and policemen on their
    beats
And cats, but else deserted; now I miss
That lively mind and guttural laugh of his
And that strange way he had of making
    gleam,
Like something real, the art we used to
    dream.

London has been my prison; but my books

Hills and great waters, labouring men and
    brooks,

Ships and deep friendships and remembered
    days

Which even now set all my mind ablaze

As that June day when, in the red bricks'
    chinks

I saw the old Roman ruins white with
    pinks

And felt the hillside haunted even then

By not dead memory of the Roman men.

And felt the hillside thronged by souls un-
    seen

Who knew the interest in me and were keen

That man alive should understand man
    dead

So many centuries since the blood was shed.

And quickened with strange hush because
    this comer

Sensed a strange soul alive behind the
    summer.

That other day on Ercall when the stones
Were sunbleached white, like long unburied
    bones,

While the bees droned and all the air was
    sweet

From honey buried underneath my feet,
Honey of purple heather and white clover
Sealed in its gummy bags till summer's
    over.

Then other days by water, by bright sea,
Clear as clean glass and my bright friend
    with me,

The cove clean bottomed where we saw the
    brown

Red spotted plaice go skimming six feet
    down

And saw the long fronds waving, white
    with shells,

Waving, unfolding, drooping, to the swells;

That sadder day when we beheld the great

And terrible beauty of a Lammas spate

Roaring white-mouthed in all the great
     cliff's gaps

Headlong, tree-tumbling fury of collapse,

While drenching clouds drove by and every
     sense

Was water roaring or rushing or in offence,

And mountain sheep stood huddled and
     blown gaps gleamed

Where torn white hair of torrents shook
     and streamed.

That sadder day when we beheld again

A spate going down in sunshine after rain,

When the blue reach of water leaping
     bright

Was one long ripple and clatter, flecked
     with white.

And that far day, that never blotted page

When youth was bright like flowers about
      old age
Fair generations bringing thanks for life
To that old kindly man and trembling wife
After their sixty years: Time never made
A better beauty since the Earth was laid
Than that thanksgiving given to grey hair
For the great gift of life which brought
      them there.

Days of endeavour have been good: the
      days
Racing in cutters for the comrade's praise,
The day they led my cutter at the turn
Yet could not keep the lead and dropped
      astern,
The moment in the spurt when both boats'
      oars
Dipped in each other's wash and throats
      grew hoarse

And teeth ground into teeth and both
    strokes quickened

Lashing the sea, and gasps came, and hearts
    sickened

And coxswains damned us, dancing, banking
    stroke,

To put our weights on, though our hearts
    were broke

And both boats seemed to stick and sea
    seemed glue,

The tide a mill race we were struggling
    through

And every quick recover gave us squints

Of them still there, and oar tossed water-
    glints

And cheering came, our friends, our foemen
    cheering,

A long, wild, rallying murmur on the hear-
    ing—

"Port Fore!" and "Starboard Fore!"
    "Port Fore." "Port Fore."

"Up with her, Starboard," and at that each
    oar
Lightened, though arms were bursting, and
    eyes shut
And the oak stretchers grunted in the strut
And the curse quickened from the cox, our
    bows
Crashed, and drove talking water, we made
    vows
Chastity vows and temperance; in our pain
We numbered things we'd never eat again
If we could only win; then came the yell
"Starboard," "Port Fore," and then a
    beaten bell
Rung as for fire to cheer us. "Now."
    Oars bent
Soul took the looms now body's bolt was
    spent,
"Damn it, come on now," "On now,"
    "On now," "Starboard."

"Port Fore." "Up with her, Port"; each
cutter harboured

Ten eye-shut painsick strugglers, "Heave,
oh, heave,"

Catcalls waked echoes like a shrieking
sheave.

"Heave," and I saw a back, then two.
"Port Fore."

"Starboard." "Come on." I saw the mid-
ship oar

And knew we had done them. "Port Fore."
"Starboard." "Now."

I saw bright water spurting at their bow

Their cox' full face an instant. They were
done.

The watchers' cheering almost drowned the
gun.

We had hardly strength to toss our oars;
our cry

Cheering the losing cutter was a sigh.

Other bright days of action have seemed
    great :
Wild days in a pampero off the Plate ;
Good swimming days, at Hog Back or the
    Coves
Which the young gannet and the corbie
    loves ;
Surf-swimming between rollers, catching
    breath
Between the advancing grave and breaking
    death,
Then shooting up into the sunbright smooth
To watch the advancing roller bare her tooth,
And days of labour also, loading, hauling ;
Long days at winch or capstan, heaving,
    pawling ;
The days with oxen, dragging stone from
    blasting,
And dusty days in mills, and hot days
    masting.

Trucking on dust-dry deckings smooth like
    ice,
And hunts in mighty wool-racks after mice;
Mornings with buckwheat when the fields
    did blanch
With White Leghorns come from the chicken
    ranch.
Days near the spring upon the sunburnt hill,
Plying the maul or gripping tight the drill.
Delights of work most real, delights that
    change
The headache life of towns to rapture
    strange
Not known by townsmen, nor imagined;
    health
That puts new glory upon mental wealth
And makes the poor man rich.

               But that ends, too,
Health with its thoughts of life; and that
    bright view

That sunny landscape from life's peak, that
      glory,

And all a glad man's comments on life's
      story

And thoughts of marvellous towns and liv-
      ing men

And what pens tell and all beyond the pen

End, and are summed in words so truly
      dead

They raise no image of the heart and head,

The life, the man alive, the friend we knew,

The mind ours argued with or listened to,

None; but are dead, and all life's keenness,
      all,

Is dead as print before the funeral,

Even deader after, when the dates are
      sought,

And cold minds disagree with what we
      thought.

This many pictured world of many passions

Wears out the nations as a woman fashions,

And what life is is much to very few,

Men being so strange, so mad, and what
　　　men do

So good to watch or share; but when men
　　　count

Those hours of life that were a bursting
　　　fount,

Sparkling the dusty heart with living
　　　springs,

There seems a world, beyond our earthly
　　　things,

Gated by golden moments, each bright
　　　time

Opening to show the city white like lime,

High towered and many peopled. This
　　　made sure,

Work that obscures those moments seems
　　　impure,

Making our not-returning time of breath

Dull with the ritual and records of death,

That frost of fact by which our wisdom
   gives

Correctly stated death to all that lives.

Best trust the happy moments. What they
   gave

Makes man less fearful of the certain grave,

And gives his work compassion and new
   eyes.

The days that make us happy make us wise.

SHIPS

I CANNOT tell their wonder nor make known
Magic that once thrilled through me to the
     bone,
But all men praise some beauty, tell some
     tale,
Vent a high mood which makes the rest
     seem pale,
Pour their heart's blood to flourish one
     green leaf,
Follow some Helen for her gift of grief,
And fail in what they mean, whate'er they
     do:
You should have seen, man cannot tell to
     you
The beauty of the ships of that my city.

That beauty now is spoiled by the sea's pity;

For one may haunt the pier a score of
    times,

Hearing St. Nicholas bells ring out the
    chimes,

Yet never see those proud ones swaying
    home

With mainyards backed and bows a cream
    of foam,

Those bows so lovely-curving, cut so fine,

Those coulters of the many-bubbled brine,

As once, long since, when all the docks were
    filled

With that sea-beauty man has ceased to
    build.

Yet, though their splendour may have
    ceased to be,

Each played her sovereign part in making
    me;

Now I return my thanks with heart and
    lips
For the great queenliness of all those ships.

And first the first bright memory, still so
    clear,
An autumn evening in a golden year,
When in the last lit moments before dark
The *Chepica*, a steel-grey lovely barque,
Came to an anchor near us on the flood,
Her trucks aloft in sun-glow red as blood.

Then come so many ships that I could
    fill
Three docks with their fair hulls remem-
    bered still,
Each with her special memory's special
    grace,
Riding the sea, making the waves give
    place

To delicate high beauty; man's best
    strength,
Noble in every line in all their length.
Ailsa, Genista, ships, with long jibbooms,
The *Wanderer* with great beauty and strange
    dooms,
Liverpool (mightiest then) superb, sublime,
The *California* huge, as slow as time.
The *Copley* swift, the perfect *J. T. North,*
The loveliest barque my city has sent forth,
Dainty *John Lockett* well remembered yet,
The splendid *Argus* with her skysail set,
Stalwart *Drumcliff,* white-blocked, majestic
    Sierras,
Divine bright ships, the water's standard-
    bearers;
Melpomene, Euphrosyne, and their sweet
Sea-troubling sisters of the Fernie fleet;
Corunna (in whom my friend died) and the
    old

Long since loved *Esmeralda* long since
    sold.

Centurion passed in Rio, *Glaucus* spoken,

Aladdin burnt, the *Bidston* water-broken,

Yola, in whom my friend sailed, *Dawpool*
    trim,

Fierce-bowed *Egeria* plunging to the swim,

Stanmore wide-sterned, sweet *Cupica*, tall
        Bard,

Queen in all harbours with her moon sail
    yard.

Though I tell many, there must still be
    others,

McVickar Marshall's ships and Fernie
    Brothers',

Lochs, *Counties*, *Shires*, *Drums*, the count-
    less lines

Whose house-flags all were once familiar
    signs

At high main-trucks on Mersey's windy
    ways
When sunlight made the wind-white water
    blaze.
Their names bring back old mornings, when
    the docks
Shone with their house-flags and their
    painted blocks,
Their raking masts below the Custom
    House
And all the marvellous beauty of their
    bows.

Familiar steamers, too, majestic steamers,
Shearing Atlantic roller-tops to streamers,
Umbria, Etruria, noble, still at sea,
The grandest, then, that man had brought
    to be.
Majestic, City of Paris, City of Rome,
Forever jealous racers, out and home.

The *Alfred Holt's* blue smoke-stacks down
the stream,

The fair *Loanda* with her bows a-cream.

Booth liners, Anchor liners, Red Star liners,

The marks and styles of countless ship-
designers,

The *Magdalena, Puno, Potosi*,

Lost *Cotopaxi*, all well known to me.

These splendid ships, each with her grace,
her glory,

Her memory of old song or comrade's story,

Still in my mind the image of life's need,

Beauty in hardest action, beauty indeed.

"They built great ships and sailed them"
sounds most brave

Whatever arts we have or fail to have;

I touch my country's mind, I come to grips

With half her purpose, thinking of these
ships

That art untouched by softness, all that
line

Drawn ringing hard to stand the test of
brine,

That nobleness and grandeur, all that
beauty

Born of a manly life and bitter duty,

That splendour of fine bows which yet
could stand

The shock of rollers never checked by land.

That art of masts, sail crowded, fit to break,

Yet stayed to strength and backstayed
into rake,

The life demanded by that art, the keen

Eye-puckered, hard-case seamen, silent,
lean, —

They are grander things than all the art of
towns,

Their tests are tempests and the sea that
drowns,

They are my country's line, her great art
    done
By strong brains labouring on the thought
    unwon,
They mark our passage as a race of men,
Earth will not see such ships as those again.

TRUTH

Man with his burning soul
Has but an hour of breath
To build a ship of Truth
In which his soul may sail,
Sail on the sea of death.
For death takes toll
Of beauty, courage, youth,
Of all but Truth.

Life's city ways are dark,
Men mutter by; the wells
Of the great waters moan.
O death, O sea, O tide,
The waters moan like bells.
No light, no mark,
The soul goes out alone
On seas unknown.

Stripped of all purple robes,
Stripped of all golden lies,
I will not be afraid.
Truth will preserve through death;
Perhaps the stars will rise,
The stars like globes.
The ship my striving made
May see night fade.

THEY CLOSED HER EYES

FROM THE SPANISH OF DON GUSTAVO
A. BÉCQUER.

THEY closed her eyes,

They were still open;

They hid her face

With a white linen,

And, some sobbing,

Others in silence,

From the sad bedroom

All came away.

The night-light in a dish

Burned on the floor,

It flung on the wall

The bed's shadow,

And in that shadow
One saw sometimes
Drawn in sharp line
The body's shape.

The day awakened
At its first whiteness
With its thousand noises;
The town awoke
Before that contrast
Of life and strangeness,
Of light and darkness.
I thought a moment
   My God, how lonely
   The dead are!

From the house, shoulder-high
To church they bore her,
And in a chapel
They left her bier.

There they surrounded
Her pale body
With yellow candles
And black stuffs.

At the last stroke
Of the ringing for the souls
An old crone finished
Her last prayers.
She crossed the narrow nave;
The doors moaned,
And the holy place
Remained deserted.

From a clock one heard
The measured ticking,
And from some candles
The guttering.
All things there
Were so grim and sad,

So dark and rigid,

That I thought a moment,

  My God, how lonely

  The dead are!

From the high belfry

The tongue of iron

Clanged, giving out

His sad farewell.

Crape on their clothes,

Her friends and kindred

Passed in a row,

Making procession.

In the last vault,

Dark and narrow,

The pickaxe opened

A niche at one end;

There they laid her down.

Soon they bricked the place up,

And with a gesture
Bade grief farewell.

Pickaxe on shoulder
The grave-digger,
Singing between his teeth,
Passed out of sight.
The night came down;
It was all silent,
Lost in the shadows
I thought a moment.
　　My God, how lonely
　　The dead are!

In the long nights
Of bitter winter,
When the wind makes
The rafters creak,
When the violent rain
Lashes the windows,
Lonely, I remember
That poor girl.

There falls the rain
With its noise eternal.
There the north wind
Fights with the rain.
Stretched in the hollow
Of the damp bricks
Perhaps her bones
Freeze with the cold.

Does the dust return to dust?
Does the soul fly to heaven?
Is all vile matter,
Rottenness, filthiness?
I know not. But
There is something — something
That I cannot explain,
Something that gives us
Loathing, terror,
To leave the dead
So alone, so wretched.

THE HARP

FROM THE SPANISH OF DON GUSTAVO
A. BECQUER

In a dark corner of the room,
Perhaps forgotten by its owner,
Silent and dim with dust,
I saw the harp.

How many musics slumbered in its strings,
As the bird sleeps in the branches,
Waiting the snowy hand
That could awaken them.

Ah me, I thought, how many, many times
Genius thus slumbers in a human soul,
Waiting, as Lazarus waited, for a voice
To bid him "Rise and walk."

SONNET

FROM THE SPANISH OF DON FRANCISCO DE
QUEVEDO

I saw the ramparts of my native land,

One time so strong, now dropping in decay,

Their strength destroyed by this new age's
way

That has worn out and rotted what was
grand.

I went into the fields: there I could see

The sun drink up the waters newly thawed,

And on the hills the moaning cattle pawed;

Their miseries robbed the day of light for
me.

I went into my house: I saw how spotted,

Decaying things made that old home their
prize.

My withered walking-staff had come to
  bend;
I felt the age had won; my sword was
  rotted,
And there was nothing on which I set my
  eyes
That was not a reminder of the end.

SONNET ON THE DEATH OF HIS WIFE

FROM THE PORTUGUESE OF ANTONIO DE
FERREIRO

THAT blessed sunlight that once showed to
    me
My way to heaven more plain more cer-
    tainly,
And with her bright beam banished utterly
All trace of mortal sorrow far from me,
Has gone from me, has left her prison sad,
And I am blind and alone and gone astray,
Like a lost pilgrim in a desert way
Wanting the blessed guide that once he had.

Thus with a spirit bowed and mind a blur
I trace the holy steps where she has gone,

By valleys and by meadows and by moun-
    tains,
And everywhere I catch a glimpse of her.
She takes me by the hand and leads me on,
And my eyes follow her, my eyes made
    fountains.

SONG

ONE sunny time in May
When lambs were sporting,
The sap ran in the spray
And I went courting,
And all the apple boughs
Were bright with blossom,
I picked an early rose
For my love's bosom.

And then I met her friend,
Down by the water,
Who cried "She's met her end,
That gray-eyed daughter;
That voice of hers is stilled
Her beauty broken."
O me, my love is killed,
My love unspoken.

She was too sweet, too dear,
To die so cruel,
O Death, why leave me here
And take my jewel?
Her voice went to the bone,
So true, so ringing,
And now I go alone,
Winter or springing.

THE BALLAD OF SIR BORS

Would I could win some quiet and rest, and
    a little ease,
In the cool grey hush of the dusk, in the
    dim green place of the trees,
Where the birds are singing, singing, sing-
    ing, crying aloud
The song of the red, red rose that blossoms
    beyond the seas.

Would I could see it, the rose, when the
    light begins to fail,
And a lone white star in the West is glim-
    mering on the mail;
The red, red passionate rose of the sacred
    blood of the Christ,
In the shining chalice of God, the cup of
    the Holy Grail.

The dusk comes gathering grey, and the
　　darkness dims the West,
The oxen low to the byre, and all bells ring
　　to rest;
But I ride over the moors, for the dusk still
　　bides and waits,
That brims my soul with the glow of the
　　rose that ends the Quest.

My horse is spavined and ribbed, and his
　　bones come through his hide,
My sword is rotten with rust, but I shake
　　the reins and ride,
For the bright white birds of God that nest
　　in the rose have called,
And never a township now is a town where
　　I can bide.

It will happen at last, at dusk, as my horse
　　limps down the fell,

A star will glow like a note God strikes on a
    silver bell,
And the bright white birds of God will
    carry my soul to Christ,
And the sight of the Rose, the Rose, will
    pay for the years of hell.

SPANISH WATERS

Spanish waters, Spanish waters, you are
    ringing in my ears,
Like a slow sweet piece of music from the
    grey forgotten years;
Telling tales, and beating tunes, and bring-
    ing weary thoughts to me
Of the sandy beach at Muertos, where I
    would that I could be.

There's a surf breaks on Los Muertos, and
    it never stops to roar,
And it's there we came to anchor, and it's
    there we went ashore,
Where the blue lagoon is silent amid snags
    of rotting trees,
Dropping like the clothes of corpses cast up
    by the seas.

We anchored at Los Muertos when the dip-
    ping sun was red,
We left her half-a-mile to sea, to west of
    Nigger Head;
And before the mist was on the Cay, before
    the day was done,
We were all ashore on Muertos with the
    gold that we had won.

We bore it through the marshes in a half-
    score battered chests,
Sinking, in the sucking quagmires, to the
    sunburn on our breasts,
Heaving over tree-trunks, gasping, damning
    at the flies and heat,
Longing for a long drink, out of silver, in
    the ship's cool lazareet.

The moon came white and ghostly as we
    laid the treasure down,

There was gear there'd make a beggarman
    as rich as Lima Town,
Copper charms and silver trinkets from the
    chests of Spanish crews,
Gold doubloons and double moydores, louis
    d'ors and portagues,

Clumsy yellow-metal earrings from the
    Indians of Brazil,
Uncut emeralds out of Rio, bezoar stones
    from Guayaquil;
Silver, in the crude and fashioned, pots of
    old Arica bronze,
Jewels from the bones of Incas desecrated
    by the Dons.

We smoothed the place with mattocks, and
    we took and blazed the tree,
Which marks yon where the gear is hid that
    none will ever see,

And we laid aboard the ship again, and
    south away we steers,
Through the loud surf of Los Muertos
    which is beating in my ears.

I'm the last alive that knows it. All the
    rest have gone their ways
Killed, or died, or come to anchor in the old
    Mulatas Cays,
And I go singing, fiddling, old and starved
    and in despair,
And I know where all that gold is hid, if I
    were only there.

It's not the way to end it all. I'm old,
    and nearly blind,
And an old man's past's a strange thing,
    for it never leaves his mind.
And I see in dreams, awhiles, the beach,
    the sun's disc dipping red,

And the tall ship, under topsails, swaying
      in past Nigger Head.

I'd be glad to step ashore there. Glad to
      take a pick and go
To the lone blazed coco-palm tree in the
      place no others know,
And lift the gold and silver that has
      mouldered there for years
By the loud surf of Los Muertos which is
      beating in my ears.

CARGOES

Quinquireme of Nineveh from distant
    Ophir,
Rowing home to haven in sunny Palestine,
With a cargo of ivory,
And apes and peacocks,
Sandalwood, cedarwood, and sweet white
    wine.

Stately Spanish galleon coming from the
    Isthmus,
Dipping through the Tropics by the palm-
    green shores,
With a cargo of diamonds,
Emeralds, amethysts,
Topazes, and cinnamon, and gold moidores.

Dirty British coaster with a salt-caked
smoke stack,

Butting through the Channel in the mad
March days,

With a cargo of Tyne coal,

Road-rails, pig-lead,

Firewood, iron-ware, and cheap tin trays.

CAPTAIN STRATTON'S FANCY

Oh some are fond of red wine, and some are
    fond of white,
And some are all for dancing by the pale
    moonlight;
But rum alone's the tipple, and the heart's
    delight
  Of the old bold mate of Henry Morgan.

Oh some are fond of Spanish wine, and
    some are fond of French,
And some'll swallow tay and stuff fit only
    for a wench;
But I'm for right Jamaica till I roll beneath
    the bench,
  Says the old bold mate of Henry Morgan.

Oh some are for the lily, and some are for
the rose,

But I am for the sugar-cane that in Jamaica
grows;

For it's that that makes the bonny drink to
warm my copper nose,

Says the old bold mate of Henry Morgan.

Oh some are fond of fiddles, and a song
well sung,

And some are all for music for to lilt upon
the tongue;

But mouths were made for tankards, and
for sucking at the bung,

Says the old bold mate of Henry Morgan.

Oh some are fond of dancing, and some are
fond of dice,

And some are all for red lips, and pretty
lasses' eyes;

But a right Jamaica puncheon is a finer
    prize
  To the old bold mate of Henry Morgan.

Oh some that's good and godly ones they
    hold that it's a sin
To troll the jolly bowl around, and let the
    dollars spin;
But I'm for toleration and for drinking at
    an inn,
  Says the old bold mate of Henry Morgan.

Oh some are sad and wretched folk that go
    in silken suits,
And there's a mort of wicked rogues that
    live in good reputes;
So I'm for drinking honestly, and dying in
    my boots,
  Like an old bold mate of Henry Morgan.

AN OLD SONG RE–SUNG

I saw a ship a-sailing, a-sailing, a-sailing,

With emeralds and rubies and sapphires in
her hold;

And a bosun in a blue coat bawling at the
railing,

Piping through a silver call that had a chain
of gold;

The summer wind was failing and the tall
ship rolled.

I saw a ship a-steering, a-steering,
a-steering,

With roses in red thread worked upon her
sails;

With sacks of purple amethysts, the spoils
of buccaneering,

Skins of musky yellow wine, and silks in
  bales,
Her merry men were cheering, hauling on
  the brails.

I saw a ship a-sinking, a-sinking, a-sinking,
With glittering sea-water splashing on her
  decks,
With seamen in her spirit-room singing
  songs and drinking,
Pulling claret bottles down, and knocking
  off the necks,
The broken glass was chinking as she sank
  among the wrecks.

ST. MARY'S BELLS

IT'S pleasant in Holy Mary
By San Marie lagoon,
The bells they chime and jingle
From dawn to afternoon.
They rhyme and chime and mingle,
They pulse and boom and beat,
And the laughing bells are gentle
And the mournful bells are sweet.

Oh, who are the men that ring them,
The bells of San Marie,
Oh, who but sonsie seamen
Come in from over sea,
And merrily in the belfries
They rock and sway and hale,
And send the bells a-jangle,
And down the lusty ale.

It's pleasant in Holy Mary
To hear the beaten bells
Come booming into music,
Which throbs, and clangs, and swells,
From sunset till the daybreak,
From dawn to afternoon.
In port of Holy Mary
On San Marie lagoon.

LONDON TOWN

Oн London Town's a fine town, and Lon-
      don sights are rare,
And London ale is right ale, and brisk's the
      London air,
And busily goes the world there, but crafty
      grows the mind,
And London Town of all towns I'm glad to
      leave behind.

Then hey for croft and hop-yard, and hill,
      and field, and pond,
With Breden Hill before me and Malvern
      Hill beyond.
The hawthorn white i' the hedgerow, and
      all the spring's attire
In the comely land of Teme and Lugg, and
      Clent, and Clee, and Wyre.

Oh London girls are brave girls, in silk and
     cloth o' gold,
And London shops are rare shops, where
     gallant things are sold,
And bonnily clinks the gold there, but
     drowsily blinks the eye,
And London Town of all towns I'm glad to
     hurry by.

Then, hey for covert and woodland, and
     ash and elm and oak,
Tewkesbury inns, and Malvern roofs, and
     Worcester chimney smoke,
The apple trees in the orchard, the cattle in
     the byre,
And all the land from Ludlow town to
     Bredon church's spire.

Oh London tunes are new tunes, and Lon-
     don books are wise,

And London plays are rare plays, and fine
    to country eyes,
But craftily fares the knave there, and
    wickedly fares the Jew,
And London Town of all towns I'm glad to
    hurry through.

So hey for the road, the west road, by mill
    and forge and fold,
Scent of the fern and song of the lark by
    brook, and field, and wold,
To the comely folk at the hearth-stone and
    the talk beside the fire,
In the hearty land, where I was bred, my
    land of heart's desire.

THE EMIGRANT

GOING by Daly's shanty I heard the boys
within
Dancing the Spanish hornpipe to Driscoll's
violin,
I heard the sea-boots shaking the rough
planks of the floor,
But I was going westward, I hadn't heart
for more.

All down the windy village the noise rang
in my ears,
Old sea boots stamping, shuffling, it brought
the bitter tears,
The old tune piped and quavered, the lilts
came clear and strong,
But I was going westward, I couldn't join
the song.

There were the grey stone houses, the night
    wind blowing keen,
The hill-sides pale with moonlight, the
    young corn springing green,
The hearth nooks lit and kindly, with dear
    friends good to see,
But I was going westward, and the ship
    waited me.

PORT OF HOLY PETER

THE blue laguna rocks and quivers,
　　Dull gurgling eddies twist and spin,
The climate does for people's livers,
　　It's a nasty place to anchor in
　　　　Is Spanish port,
　　　　Fever port,
　　　　Port of Holy Peter.

The town begins on the sea-beaches,
　　And the town's mad with the stinging
　　　　flies,
The drinking water's mostly leeches,
　　It's a far remove from Paradise
　　　　Is Spanish port,
　　　　Fever port,
　　　　Port of Holy Peter.

There's sand-bagging and throat-slitting,
   And quiet graves in the sea slime,
Stabbing, of course, and rum-hitting,
   Dirt, and drink, and stink, and crime,
      In Spanish port,
      Fever port,
      Port of Holy Peter.

All the day the wind's blowing
   From the sick swamp below the hills,
All the night the plague's growing,
   And the dawn brings the fever chills,
      In Spanish port,
      Fever port,
      Port of Holy Peter.

You get a thirst there's no slaking,
   You get the chills and fever-shakes,
Tongue yellow and head aching,
   And then the sleep that never wakes.

And all the year the heat's baking,
The sea rots and the earth quakes,
In Spanish port,
Fever port,
Port of Holy Peter.

BEAUTY

I HAVE seen dawn and sunset on moors and
    windy hills
Coming in solemn beauty like slow old
    tunes of Spain:
I have seen the lady April bringing the
    daffodils,
Bringing the springing grass and the soft
    warm April rain.

I have heard the song of the blossoms and
    the old chant of the sea,
And seen strange lands from under the
    arched white sails of ships;
But the loveliest things of beauty God ever
    has showed to me,
Are her voice, and her hair, and eyes, and
    the dear red curve of her lips.

THE SEEKERS

Friends and loves we have none, nor
wealth nor blessed abode,
But the hope of the City of God at the
other end of the road.

Not for us are content, and quiet, and peace
of mind,
For we go seeking a city that we shall never
find.

There is no solace on earth for us — for
such as we —
Who search for a hidden city that we shall
never see.

Only the road and the dawn, the sun, the
      wind, and the rain,
And the watch fire under stars, and sleep,
      and the road again.

We seek the City of God, and the haunt
      where beauty dwells,
And we find the noisy mart and the sound
      of burial bells.

Never the golden city, where radiant people
      meet,
But the dolorous town where mourners are
      going about the street.

We travel the dusty road till the light of
      the day is dim,
And sunset shows us spires away on the
      world's rim.

We travel from dawn to dusk, till the day
     is past and by,
Seeking the Holy City beyond the rim of
     the sky.

Friends and loves we have none, nor wealth
     nor blest abode,
But the hope of the City of God at the
     other end of the road.

PRAYER

When the last sea is sailed, when the last shallow's charted,

When the last field is reaped, and the last harvest stored,

When the last fire is out and the last guest departed,

Grant the last prayer that I shall pray, be good to me, O Lord.

And let me pass in a night at sea, a night of storm and thunder,

In the loud crying of the wind through sail and rope and spar,

Send me a ninth great peaceful wave to drown and roll me under

To the cold tunny-fish's home where the drowned galleons are.

241

And in the dim green quiet place far out of
      sight and hearing,
Grant I may hear at whiles the wash and
      thresh of the sea-foam
About the fine keen bows of the stately
      clippers steering
Towards the lone northern star and the fair
      ports of home.

DAWN

THE dawn comes cold: the haystack smokes,
　The green twigs crackle in the fire,
The dew is dripping from the oaks,
And sleepy men bear milking-yokes
　Slowly towards the cattle-byre.

Down in the town a clock strikes six,
　The grey east heaven burns and glows,
The dew shines on the thatch of ricks,
A slow old crone comes gathering sticks,
　The red cock in the ox-yard crows.

Beyond the stack where we have lain
　The road runs twisted like a snake
(The white road to the land of Spain),
The road that we must foot again,
　Though the feet halt and the heart ache.

LAUGH AND BE MERRY

LAUGH and be merry, remember, better the
world with a song,
Better the world with a blow in the teeth of
a wrong.
Laugh, for the time is brief, a thread the
length of a span.
Laugh and be proud to belong to the old
proud pageant of man.

Laugh and be merry: remember, in olden
time.
God made Heaven and Earth for joy He
took in a rhyme,
Made them, and filled them full with the
strong red wine of His mirth,
The splendid joy of the stars: the joy of
the earth.

So we must laugh and drink from the deep
    blue cup of the sky,
Join the jubilant song of the great stars
    sweeping by,
Laugh, and battle, and work, and drink of the
    wine outpoured
In the dear green earth, the sign of the joy
    of the Lord.

Laugh and be merry together, like brothers
    akin,
Guesting awhile in the rooms of a beautiful
    inn,
Glad till the dancing stops, and the lilt of
    the music ends.
Laugh till the game is played; and be you
    merry, my friends.

JUNE TWILIGHT

THE twilight comes; the sun
   Dips down and sets,
The boys have done
   Play at the nets.

In a warm golden glow
   The woods are steeped.
The shadows grow;
   The bat has cheeped.

Sweet smells the new-mown hay;
   The mowers pass
Home, each his way,
   Through the grass.

The night-wind stirs the fern,
  A night-jar spins;
The windows burn
  In the inns.

Dusky it grows. The moon!
  The dews descend.
Love, can this beauty in our hearts
  End?

ROADWAYS

ONE road leads to London,
  One road runs to Wales,
My road leads me seawards
  To the white dipping sails.

One road leads to the river,
  As it goes singing slow;
My road leads to shipping,
  Where the bronzed sailors go.

Leads me, lures me, calls me
  To salt green tossing sea;
A road without earth's road-dust
  Is the right road for me.

A wet road heaving, shining,
  And wild with seagulls' cries,
248

A mad salt sea-wind blowing
The salt spray in my eyes.

My road calls me, lures me
West, east, south, and north;
Most roads lead men homewards,
My road leads me forth

To add more miles to the tally
Of grey miles left behind,
In quest of that one beauty
God put me here to find.

MIDSUMMER NIGHT

THE perfect disc of the sacred moon
   Through still blue heaven serenely swims,
   And the lone bird's liquid music brims
The peace of the night with a perfect tune.

This is that holiest night of the year
   When (the mowers say) may be heard and
      seen
   The ghostly court of the English queen,
Who rides to harry and hunt the deer.

And the woodland creatures cower awake,
   A strange unrest is on harts and does,
   For the maiden Dian a-hunting goes,
And the trembling deer are afoot in the
      brake.

They start at a shaken leaf: the sound
　Of a dry twig snapped by a squirrel's foot
　Is a nameless dread: and to them the
　　　hoot
Of a mousing owl is the cry of a hound.

Oh soon the forest will ring with cries,
　The dim green coverts will flash: the
　　　grass
　Will glow as the radiant hunters pass
After the quarry with burning eyes.

The hurrying feet will range unstayed
　Of questing goddess and hunted fawn,
　Till the east is grey with the sacred dawn,
And the red cock wakens the milking maid.

THE HARPER'S SONG

This sweetness trembling from the strings
 The music of my troublous lute
 Hath timed Herodias' daughter's foot;
Setting a-clink her ankle-rings
Whenas she danced to feasted kings.

Where gemmed apparel burned and caught
 The sunset 'neath the golden dome,
 To the dark beauties of old Rome
My sorrowful lute hath haply brought
Sad memories sweet with tender thought.

When night had fallen and lights and fires
 Were darkened in the homes of men,
 Some sighing echo stirred: — and then
The old cunning wakened from the wires
The old sorrows and the old desires.

252

Dead Kings in long forgotten lands,
  And all dead beauteous women; some
  Whose pride imperial hath become
Old armour rusting in the sands
And shards of iron in dusty hands,

Have heard my lyre's soft rise and fall
  Go trembling down the paven ways,
  Till every heart was all ablaze —
Hasty each foot — to obey the call
To triumph or to funeral.

Could I begin again the slow
  Sweet mournful music filled with tears,
  Surely the old, dead, dusty ears
Would hear; the old drowsy eyes would
      glow,
Old memories come; old hopes and fears,
And time restore the long ago.

THE GENTLE LADY

So beautiful, so dainty-sweet,
So like a lyre's delightful touch —
A beauty perfect, ripe, complete
That art's own hand could only smutch
And nature's self not better much.

So beautiful, so purely wrought,
Like a fair missal penned with hymns,
So gentle, so surpassing thought —
A beauteous soul in lovely limbs,
A lantern that an angel trims.

So simple-sweet, without a sin,
Like gentle music gently timed,
Like rhyme-words coming aptly in,
To round a moonéd poem rhymed
To tunes the laughing bells have chimed.

THE DEAD KNIGHT

THE cleanly rush of the mountain air,
And the mumbling, grumbling humble-bees,
Are the only things that wander there.
The pitiful bones are laid at ease,
The grass has grown in his tangled hair,
And a rambling bramble binds his knees.

To shrieve his soul from the pangs of hell,
The only requiem bells that rang
Were the harebell and the heather bell.
Hushed he is with the holy spell
In the gentle hymn the wind sang,
And he lies quiet, and sleeps well.
He is bleached and blanched with the sum-
    mer sun;
The misty rain and the cold dew

Have altered him from the kingly one
Whom his lady loved, and his men knew,
And dwindled him to a skeleton.

The vetches have twined about his bones,
The straggling ivy twists and creeps
In his eye-sockets: the nettle keeps
Vigil about him while he sleeps.
Over his body the wind moans
With a dreary tune throughout the day,
In a chorus wistful, eerie, thin
As the gulls' cry, as the cry in the bay,
The mournful word the seas say
When tides are wandering out or in.

SORROW OF MYDATH

WEARY the cry of the wind is, weary the
    sea,
Weary the heart and the mind and the
    body of me,
Would I were out of it, done with it, would
    I could be
  A white gull crying along the desolate
    sands.

Outcast, derelict soul in a body accurst,
Standing drenched with the spindrift, stand-
    ing athirst,
For the cool green waves of death to arise
    and burst
  In a tide of quiet for me on the desolate
    sands.

Would that the waves and the long white
    hair of the spray
Would gather in splendid terror, and blot
    me away
To the sunless place of the wrecks where
    the waters sway
  Gently, dreamily, quietly over desolate
    sands.

TWILIGHT

Twilight it is, and the far woods are dim,
and the rooks cry and call.
Down in the valley the lamps, and the mist,
and a star over all,
There by the rick, where they thresh, is the
drone at an end,
Twilight it is, and I travel the road with
my friend.

I think of the friends who are dead, who
were dear long ago in the past,
Beautiful friends who are dead, though I
know that death cannot last;
Friends with the beautiful eyes that the dust
has defiled,
Beautiful souls who were gentle when I was
a child.

INVOCATION

O WANDERER into many brains,
O spark the emperor's purple hides,
You sow the dusk with fiery grains
When the gold horseman rides.
  O beauty on the darkness hurled,
  Be it through me you shame the world.

POSTED AS MISSING

UNDER all her topsails she trembled like a
stag,

The wind made a ripple in her bonny red
flag;

They cheered her from the shore and they
cheered her from the pier,

And under all her topsails she trembled like
a deer.

So she passed swaying, where the green
seas run,

Her wind-steadied topsails were stately in
the sun;

There was glitter on the water from her
red port light,

So she passed swaying, till she was out
of sight.

Long and long ago it was, a weary time
   it is,
The bones of her sailor-men are coral plants
   by this;
Coral plants, and shark-weed, and a mer-
   maid's comb,
And if the fishers net them they never
   bring them home.

It's rough on sailors' women. They have
   to mangle hard,
And stitch at dungarees till their finger-
   ends are scarred,
Thinking of the sailor-men who sang among
   the crowd,
Hoisting of her topsails when she sailed so
   proud.

A CREED

I HOLD that when a person dies
  His soul returns again to earth;
Arrayed in some new flesh-disguise
  Another mother gives him birth.
With sturdier limbs and brighter brain
The old soul takes the roads again.

Such is my own belief and trust;
  This hand, this hand that holds the pen,
Has many a hundred times been dust
  And turned, as dust, to dust again;
These eyes of mine have blinked and shone
In Thebes, in Troy, in Babylon.

All that I rightly think or do,
  Or make, or spoil, or bless, or blast,

Is curse or blessing justly due

   For sloth or effort in the past.

My life's a statement of the sum

Of vice indulged, or overcome.

I know that in my lives to be

   My sorry heart will ache and burn,

And worship, unavailingly,

   The woman whom I used to spurn,

And shake to see another have

The love I spurned, the love she gave.

And I shall know, in angry words,

   In gibes, and mocks, and many a tear,

A carrion flock of homing-birds,

   The gibes and scorns I uttered here.

The brave word that I failed to speak

Will brand me dastard on the cheek.

And as I wander on the roads

   I shall be helped and healed and blessed;

Dear words shall cheer and be as goads
  To urge to heights before unguessed.
My road shall be the road I made;
All that I gave shall be repaid.

So shall I fight, so shall I tread,
  In this long war beneath the stars;
So shall a glory wreathe my head,
  So shall I faint and show the scars,
Until this case, this clogging mould,
Be smithied all to kingly gold.

WHEN BONY DEATH

When bony Death has chilled her gentle
    blood,
  And dimmed the brightness of her wistful
    eyes,
And changed her glorious beauty into mud
  By his old skill in hateful wizardries;

When an old lichened marble strives to tell
  How sweet a grace, how red a lip was
    hers;
When rheumy grey-beards say, "I knew her
    well,"
  Showing the grave to curious worshippers;

When all the roses that she sowed in me
  Have dripped their crimson petals and
    decayed,

Leaving no greenery on any tree
 That her dear hands in my heart's garden
  laid,

Then grant, old Time, to my green mouldering skull,
These songs may keep her memory beautiful.

THE WEST WIND

It's a warm wind, the west wind, full of
    birds' cries;
I never hear the west wind but tears are in
    my eyes.
For it comes from the west lands, the old
    brown hills,
And April's in the west wind, and daffodils.

It's a fine land, the west land, for hearts as
    tired as mine,
Apple orchards blossom there, and the air's
    like wine.
There is cool green grass there, where men
    may lie at rest,
And the thrushes are in song there, fluting
    from the nest.

"Will you not come home, brother? You
  have been long away.

It's April, and blossom time, and white is
  the spray:

And bright is the sun, brother, and warm is
  the rain,

Will you not come home, brother, home to
  us again?

The young corn is green, brother, where the
  rabbits run;

It's blue sky, and white clouds, and warm
  rain and sun.

It's song to a man's soul, brother, fire to a
  man's brain,

To hear the wild bees and see the merry
  spring again.

Larks are singing in the west, brother,
  above the green wheat,

So will you not come home, brother, and
    rest your tired feet?
I've a balm for bruised hearts, brother, sleep
    for aching eyes,"
Says the warm wind, the west wind, full of
    birds' cries.

It's the white road westwards is the road I
    must tread
To the green grass, the cool grass, and rest
    for heart and head,
To the violets and the brown brooks and
    the thrushes' song
In the fine land, the west land, the land
    where I belong.

HER HEART

Her heart is always doing lovely things,
   Filling my wintry mind with simple
     flowers;
Playing sweet tunes on my untunèd strings,
   Delighting all my undelightful hours.

She plays me like a lute, what tune she will,
   No string in me but trembles at her
     touch,
Shakes into sacred music, or is still,
   Trembles or stops, or swells, her skill is
     such.
And in the dusty tavern of my soul
   Where filthy lusts drink witches' brew for
     wine,

Her gentle hand still keeps me from the
bowl,
  Still keeps me man, saves me from being
  swine.

All grace in me, all sweetness in my verse,
Is hers, is my dear girl's, and only hers.

BEING HER FRIEND

Being her friend, I do not care, not I,
How gods or men may wrong me, beat
me down;
Her word's sufficient star to travel by,
I count her quiet praise sufficient crown.

Being her friend, I do not covet gold,
Save for a royal gift to give her pleasure;
To sit with her, and have her hand to hold,
Is wealth, I think, surpassing minted
treasure.

Being her friend, I only covet art,
A white pure flame to search me as I
trace
In crooked letters from a throbbing heart
The hymn to beauty written on her face.

FRAGMENTS

TROY TOWN is covered up with weeds,
  The rabbits and the pismires brood
On broken gold, and shards, and beads
  Where Priam's ancient palace stood.

The floors of many a gallant house
  Are matted with the roots of grass;
The glow-worm and the nimble mouse
  Among her ruins flit and pass.

And there, in orts of blackened bone,
  The widowed Trojan beauties lie,
And Simois babbles over stone
  And waps and gurgles to the sky.

Once there were merry days in Troy,
  Her chimneys smoked with cooking meals,
The passing chariots did annoy
  The sunning housewives at their wheels.

And many a lovely Trojan maid
  Set Trojan lads to lovely things;
The game of life was nobly played,
  They played the game like Queens and
    Kings.

So that, when Troy had greatly passed
  In one red roaring fiery coal,
The courts the Grecians overcast
  Became a city in the soul.

In some green island of the sea,
  Where now the shadowy coral grows
In pride and pomp and empery
  The courts of old Atlantis rose.

In many a glittering house of glass
  The Atlanteans wandered there;
The paleness of their faces was
  Like ivory, so pale they were.

And hushed they were, no noise of words
  In those bright cities ever rang;
Only their thoughts, like golden birds,
  About their chambers thrilled and sang.

They knew all wisdom, for they knew
  The souls of those Egyptian Kings
Who learned, in ancient Babilu,
  The beauty of immortal things.

They knew all beauty — when they thought
  The air chimed like a stricken lyre,
The elemental birds were wrought,
  The golden birds became a fire.

And straight to busy camps and marts
  The singing flames were swiftly gone;
The trembling leaves of human hearts
  Hid boughs for them to perch upon.

And men in desert places, men
  Abandoned, broken, sick with fears,

Rose singing, swung their swords agen,
   And laughed and died among the spears.

The green and greedy seas have drowned
   That city's glittering walls and towers,
Her sunken minarets are crowned
   With red and russet water-flowers.

In towers and rooms and golden courts
   The shadowy coral lifts her sprays;
The scrawl hath gorged her broken orts,
   The shark doth haunt her hidden ways.

But, at the falling of the tide,
   The golden birds still sing and gleam,
The Atlanteans have not died,
   Immortal things still give us dream.

The dream that fires man's heart to make,
   To build, to do, to sing or say
A beauty Death can never take,
   An Adam from the crumbled clay.

BORN FOR NOUGHT ELSE

Born for nought else, for nothing but for
    this,
  To watch the soft blood throbbing in her
    throat,
To think how comely sweet her body is,
  And learn the poem of her face by rote.

Born for nought else but to attempt a
    rhyme
  That shall describe her womanhood
    aright,
And make her holy to the end of Time,
  And be my soul's acquittal in God's
    sight.

Born for nought else but to expressly mark
  The music of her dear delicious ways;

Born but to perish meanly in the dark,

    Yet born to be the man to sing her

        praise.

Born for nought else : there is a spirit tells

My lot's a King's, being born for nothing

        else.

TEWKESBURY ROAD

It is good to be out on the road, and going
    one knows not where,
  Going through meadow and village, one
    knows not whither nor why;
Through the grey light drift of the dust, in
    the keen cool rush of the air,
  Under the flying white clouds, and the
    broad blue lift of the sky.

And to halt at the chattering brook, in the
    tall green fern at the brink
  Where the harebell grows, and the gorse,
    and the foxgloves purple and white;
Where the shy-eyed delicate deer troop
    down to the brook to drink
  When the stars are mellow and large at
    the coming on of the night.

O, to feel the beat of the rain, and the
    homely smell of the earth,
  Is a tune for the blood to jig to, a joy
    past power of words;
And the blessed green comely meadows are
    all a-ripple with mirth
  At the noise of the lambs at play and the
    dear wild cry of the birds.

THE DEATH ROOMS

My soul has many an old decaying room
 Hung with the ragged arras of the past,
Where startled faces flicker in the gloom,
 And horrid whispers set the cheek aghast.

Those dropping rooms are haunted by a
  death,
 A something like a worm gnawing a
  brain,
That bids me heed what bitter lesson saith
 The blind wind beating on the window-
  pane.

None dwells in those old rooms: none ever
  can —
 I pass them through at night with hidden
  head;

Lock'd rotting rooms her eyes must never
    scan,
  Floors that her blessed feet must never
    tread.

Haunted old rooms: rooms she must never
    know,
Where death-ticks knock and mouldering
    panels glow.

IGNORANCE

SINCE I have learned Love's shining alpha-
bet,
And spelled in ink what's writ in me in
flame,
And borne her sacred image richly set
Here in my heart to keep me quit of
shame;

Since I have learned how wise and passing
wise
Is the dear friend whose beauty I extol,
And know how sweet a soul looks through
the eyes,
That are so pure a window to her soul;

Since I have learned how rare a woman
shows

As much in all she does as in her looks,
And seen the beauty of her shame the
    rose,
    And dim the beauty writ about in books ;

All I have learned, and can learn, shows me
    this —
How scant, how slight, my knowledge of
    her is.

SEA FEVER

I MUST go down to the seas again, to the
    lonely sea and the sky,
And all I ask is a tall ship and a star to
    steer her by;
And the wheel's kick and the wind's song
    and the white sail's shaking,
And a grey mist on the sea's face, and a
    grey dawn breaking,

I must go down to the seas again, for the
    call of the running tide
Is a wild call and a clear call that may not
    be denied;
And all I ask is a windy day with the white
    clouds flying,
And the flung spray and the blown spume,
    and the sea-gulls crying.

I must go down to the seas again, to the
    vagrant gypsy life,
To the gull's way and the whale's way
    where the wind's like a whetted knife;
And all I ask is a merry yarn from a laugh-
    ing fellow-rover,
And quiet sleep and a sweet dream when
    the long trick's over.

THE WATCH IN THE WOOD

When Death has laid her in his quietude,
   And dimmed the glow of her benignant
      star,
Her tired limbs shall rest within a wood,
   In a green glade where oaks and beeches
      are,

Where the shy fawns, the pretty fawns, the
      deer,
   With mild brown eyes shall view her
      spirit's husk;
The sleeping woman of her will appear,
   The maiden Dian shining through the dusk.

And, when the stars are white as twilight
      fails,
   And the green leaves are hushed, and the
      winds swoon,

The calm pure thrilling throats of nightin-
　　gales
　Shall hymn her sleeping beauty to the
　　moon.

All the woods hushed — save for a dripping
　　rose,
All the woods dim — save where a glow-
　　worm glows.

Brimming the quiet woods with holiness,
　The lone brown birds will hymn her till
　　the dawn,
The delicate, shy, dappled deer will press
　Soft pitying muzzles on her swathèd
　　lawn.

The little pretty rabbits running by.
　Will pause among the dewy grass to
　　peep,
Their thudding hearts affrighted to espy
　The maiden Dian lying there asleep.

Brown, lustrous, placid eyes of sylvan
    things
  Will wonder at the quiet in her face,
While from the thorny branch the singer
    brings
  Beauty and peace to that immortal place.

Until the grey dawn sets the woods astir
The pure birds' thrilling psalm will mourn
    for her.

C. L. M.

In the dark womb where I began
My mother's life made me a man.
Through all the months of human birth
Her beauty fed my common earth.
I cannot see, nor breathe, nor stir,
But through the death of some of her.

Down in the darkness of the grave
She cannot see the life she gave.
For all her love, she cannot tell
Whether I use it ill or well,
Nor knock at dusty doors to find
Her beauty dusty in the mind.

If the grave's gates could be undone,
She would not know her little son,
I am so grown. If we should meet

She would pass by me in the street,
Unless my soul's face let her see
My sense of what she did for me.

What have I done to keep in mind
My debt to her and womankind?
What woman's happier life repays
Her for those months of wretched days?
For all my mouthless body leeched
Ere Birth's releasing hell was reached?

What have I done, or tried, or said
In thanks to that dear woman dead?
Men triumph over women still,
Men trample women's rights at will,
And man's lust roves the world untamed.

* * * *

O grave, keep shut lest I be shamed.

WASTE

No rose but fades: no glory but must pass:
  No hue but dims: no precious silk but
    frets.
Her beauty must go underneath the grass,
  Under the long roots of the violets.

O, many glowing beauties Time has hid
  In that dark, blotting box the villain
    sends.
He covers over with a coffin-lid
  Mothers and sons, and foes and lovely
    friends.

Maids that were redly-lipped and comely-
    skinned,
  Friends that deserved a sweeter bed than
    clay,

All are as blossoms blowing down the
    wind,
  Things the old envious villain sweeps
    away.

And though the mutterer laughs and
    church bells toll,
Death brings another April to the soul.

THIRD MATE

ALL the sheets are clacking, all the blocks
        are whining,
The sails are frozen stiff and the wetted
        decks are shining;
The reef's in the topsails, and it's coming
        on to blow,
And I think of the dear girl I left long
        ago.

Grey were her eyes, and her hair was long
        and bonny,
Golden was her hair, like the wild bees'
        honey.
And I was but a dog, and a mad one to
        despise,
The gold of her hair and the grey of her
        eyes.

There's the sea before me, and my home's
　　behind me,
And beyond there the strange lands where
　　nobody will mind me,
No one but the girls with the paint upon
　　their cheeks,
Who sell away their beauty to whomsoever
　　seeks.

There'll be drink and women there, and
　　songs and laughter,
Peace from what is past and from all that
　　follows after;
And a fellow will forget how a woman lies
　　awake,
Lonely in the night watch crying for his
　　sake.

Black it blows and bad and it howls like
　　slaughter,

And the ship she shudders as she takes the
    water.
Hissing flies the spindrift like a wind-
    blown smoke,
And I think of a woman and a heart I
    broke.

THE WILD DUCK

TWILIGHT. Red in the west.

Dimness. A glow on the wood.

The teams plod home to rest.

The wild duck come to glean.

O souls not understood,

What a wild cry in the pool;

What things have the farm ducks
  seen

That they cry so — huddle and cry?

Only the soul that goes.

Eager. Eager. Flying.

Over the globe of the moon,

Over the wood that glows.

Wings linked. Necks a-strain,

A rush and a wild crying.

* * *

A cry of the long pain

In the reeds of a steel lagoon.

In a land that no man knows.

CHRISTMAS, 1903

O, THE sea breeze will be steady, and the
tall ship's going trim,
And the dark blue skies are paling, and
the white stars burning dim;
The long night watch is over, and the long
sea-roving done,
And yonder light is the Start Point light,
and yonder comes the sun.

O, we have been with the Spaniards, and
far and long on the sea;
But there are the twisted chimneys, and
the gnarled old inns on the quay.
The wind blows keen as the day breaks,
the roofs are white with the rime,
And the church-bells ring as the sun comes
up to call men in to Prime.

The church-bells rock and jangle, and there
    is peace on the earth.
Peace and good will and plenty and Christ-
    mas games and mirth.
O, the gold glints bright on the wind-vane
    as it shifts above the squire's house,
And the water of the bar of Salcombe is
    muttering about the bows.

O, the salt sea tide of Salcombe, it
    wrinkles into wisps of foam,
And the church-bells ring in Salcombe to
    ring poor sailors home.
The belfry rocks as the bells ring, the
    chimes are merry as a song,
They ring home wandering sailors who
    have been homeless long.

THE WORD

My friend, my bonny friend, when we are
 old,
 And hand in hand go tottering down the
  hill,
May we be rich in love's refinèd gold,
 May love's gold coin be current with us
  still.

May love be sweeter for the vanished
 days,
 And your most perfect beauty still as
  dear
As when your troubled singer stood at
 gaze
 In the dear March of a most sacred
  year.

May what we are be all we might have
  been,
And that potential, perfect, O my friend,
And may there still be many sheafs to
  glean
In our love's acre, comrade, till the end.

And may we find, when ended is the page,
Death but a tavern on our pilgrimage.

THE following pages are advertisements of recent important poetry published by the Macmillan Company